Analysing the Current Afghan Context

Analysing the Current Afghan Context

Edited by
Neeraj Singh Manhas

Foreword by
Maj Gen Dr Rajan Kochhar, VSM

KNOWLEDGE WORLD
KW Publishers Pvt Ltd
New Delhi

ISBN 978-93-91490-31-7 Hardback
ISBN 978-93-91490-39-3 ebook

Published in India by Kalpana Shukla

KNOWLEDGE WORLD

KW Publishers Pvt Ltd
4676/21, First Floor, Ansari Road
Daryaganj, New Delhi 110002
Phone: +91 11 43528107
Marketing: kw@kwpub.in
Editorial: production@kwpub.in
Website: www.kwpub.in

Printed and Bound in India

Dedicated to

My Father, Honorary Captain J.S. Manhas—the bravest soldier I've ever known, who was the part of Operation Pawan in Sri Lanka, Operation Vijay in Kargil, Operation Rakshak and 26/11 during the Mumbai Taj attack and also given more than 35 years of his service to his nation and still counting.

Contents

Foreword

Neeraj Singh Manhas deserves to be complimented for writing an extremely incisive and well-articulated edited book that encompasses the complete spectrum of the subject **"Analysing the Current Afghan Context."** The ideas in the book are refreshing in its specificity which takes the reader step by step towards greater understanding of perceived geostrategic situation post take-over of Afghanistan by Taliban and leads to a logical prognosis of the options available to the major superpowers to address the threats to the overall security environment. The analytical approach and engaging flow of the book is inspiring and makes it a good read for students of International Relations and Geopolitics. I have thoroughly enjoyed reading the book and find it a great combine of being interesting as also informative. Hence, I strongly advocate that it be read by Afghanistan watchers. The book based on extensive research, offered suggestions on creating a capability to meet this multi-domain challenge, which is here to stay. A definite read for all with concern for national security and building the nation's hard power. What I like most about this book is that it has a great title. Truly speaking, Pakistan's culpability in this entire episode needs to be exposed. This book provides us with the wherewithal to gain knowledge to start understanding important issues concerning all countries of South Asia. Any student of geopolitics must start with this book. It gives a great overview of Afghanistan in simple terms while covering a vast landscape. There are no complicated theories and statistics to confuse you. No rhetoric or building up an unrealistic or imaginary picture. Issues are stated as they are and analysed simplistically with basic facts and figures. It is easy to grasp and digest mentally. Every aspect which is relevant in the Indian strategic construct has been dealt with in adequate detail. I would like to christen this book as the 'go to' book on fundamentals of relations and status at this point of time. I wish all the readers the very best in their quest to read this wonderful book.

Maj Gen Dr **Rajan Kochhar,** VSM, Veteran
Former MGAOC Central Command,
Senior Advisor Defence Research and Studies (DRaS)
and Member Centre for Joint Warfare Studies (CENJOWS)

Preface

The Taliban are a mostly Pashtun, Islamic fundamentalist group that came back to power in Afghanistan in 2021 after a 20-year insurgency.

Afterwards, the Taliban regrouped across the border in Pakistan and began regaining territory less than ten years after they were ousted from power in 2001. This is what happened. At the end of August 2021, the Taliban had taken over most major cities and the capital of Afghanistan, Kabul. The group launched a quick attack as the United States began to leave Afghanistan as part of a deal with the Taliban for a peace deal in 2020.

Analysts claim that even though the Taliban said they would respect the rights of women and minorities and give amnesty to people who helped the US, they are likely to rule harshly. Meanwhile, the group is having a hard time giving Afghans security, health care, and economic opportunities.

Do the Taliban Constitute a Danger?

Experts say that the Taliban are putting Afghans' civil and political rights at risk right now because they don't like the constitution made by the US-backed government. They say that if the Taliban don't protect Afghans' rights, they could stop giving aid. This would cause a very bad humanitarian crisis. Observers also fear that the Taliban could allow terrorists to operate in Afghanistan, which could have a big impact on both regional and global security.

Since taking back control, the Taliban has done things that are similar to what they did in the late 1990s. Protesters and journalists have been arrested, beaten, and detained by the government. They have also re-established their Ministry for the Promotion of Virtue and Prevention of Vice, which was in charge of enforcing rules against un-Islamic behaviour under the Taliban. Women will be able to study at universities in gender-segregated classrooms and in Islamic clothing, the group's acting higher education minister said.

The Taliban also want to take away the progress that Afghans have made since the US invaded. There are a lot of people who say that Afghanistan is going to fall apart. There are a lot of people who say that poverty, hunger, and the economy are all going up. Hundreds of thousands of people could leave their homes and join the millions of Afghans who have already been forced to flee their homes. Some countries and international organisations have stopped giving money to help the economy and public health. This has made the crisis even worse. The country is also in the middle of a drought and the COVID-19 pandemic at the same time.

International observers are also worried that the Taliban help terrorist groups, such as Al Qaeda, which could be dangerous for both the region and the world. After Afghanistan refused to hand over Osama bin Laden, the mastermind of the 9/11 attacks, the United States went into Afghanistan to try to get them to hand him over. As long as the Taliban is in charge, Afghanistan could become a safe haven for terrorists who could attack the United States and its allies, experts say, even though the Taliban says, "Afghanistan's soil will not be used against the security of any other country."

Al Qaeda is still a big part of the Taliban, according to a report from the UN team that keeps an eye on the group in 2021. Despite this, UN experts say that the Taliban have started to "close in on Al-Qaeda" by getting information on foreign terrorist fighters and registering them. The Taliban keep giving Al Qaeda protection in exchange for money and training. There are thought to be between 200 and 500 Al Qaeda fighters in Afghanistan, and the group's leaders are thought to be living near the Afghanistan-Pakistan border. Many members of the Taliban's interim cabinet had worked with Al Qaeda in the past. Some are thought to still have ties to Al Qaeda today.

They also fight against their rival, the Islamic State in Khorasan. This group has up to 2,200 members in Afghanistan. It's likely that the terrorist group will keep attacking the country even as the Taliban fights to get rid of it. The Islamic State in Khorasan said it was behind an attack near the Kabul airport that killed 13 US service members and at least 170 Afghan civilians. The withdrawal of US troops from Afghanistan has been going on for a while now.

What will the Government of the Taliban Look Like, and How will it Work?

A hardline government was set up by the Taliban in September 2021. In the past, the Taliban said the government would be led by a religious leader and get its power from clerics. The Islamic Emirate of Afghanistan will be the name of the new government. They haven't talked about having elections. Under the US-backed government, Afghanistan was an Islamic Republic that was led by a president and based its power on universal suffrage, which is what international law and norms say. There were no women or officials from the previous government in the Taliban's cabinet. Only a few representatives from ethnic minority groups were in the cabinet. Experts say it's very unlikely that the Taliban will be able to share power with any former government officials in any real way.

The Taliban have tried to improve their diplomacy with countries in the region, like China, Pakistan, and Russia, by making more phone calls. They have told other countries and businesses to keep their embassies open and work in Afghanistan. It's still not clear what kind of relationship the United States and other Western countries will have with the Taliban. They have not yet done this. "The United States will judge [the Taliban's cabinet] by what it does," said US Secretary of State Antony Blinken. Chinese officials say that China will help Afghanistan in part if the Taliban stops terrorist activities in the area.

Who Leads the Taliban?

Taliban leaders meet every few months to make decisions about what to do. The group is called the Rahbari Shura, but it's also known as the "Quetta

Shura", because that's where Mullah Mohammed Omar and his top aides are thought to have taken refuge after the US invaded Afghanistan in 2001. Mullah Akhtar Mohammad Mansour took over from Omar when he died in 2013. Mansour was killed in a US air strike in Pakistan in 2016. "Political and military affairs" of the Emirate are decided by the council. This is what a UN monitor says. It is now led by Mawlawi Hibatullah Akhundzada, who hasn't been seen in public for a long time.

The leadership council is in charge of a number of commissions and administrative bodies that the Taliban use to run a "shadow government". Before the Taliban came to power, these bodies were called ministries. The commissions work on things like economics, education, health, and outreach. The military commission chooses "shadow governors" and "battle commanders" for each of Afghanistan's thirty-four provinces, and they are chosen by the commission. The political commission was in charge of peace talks with the United States. It has been in Doha, Qatar, for the last few years.

There are 33 people in the Taliban's new caretaker cabinet, and some of them are considered terrorists by the US and aren't welcome at the United Nations, either. Mohammad Hassan Akhund, who was good friends with Omar and had a lot of important jobs over the last two decades, is now acting prime minister, and he is in charge. Mullah Abdul Ghani Baradar, a co-founder of the Taliban and the head of the group's political commission, is Akhund's right-hand man. He is the acting minister of the interior. Sirajuddin Haqqani, who is the head of the Haqqani Network, a group of militants in Afghanistan and Pakistan that has close ties to the Taliban, Al Qaeda and Pakistan's intelligence services, runs the group. Mullah Muhammad Yaqoub, Omar's son, is in charge of the defence.

In What way did the Taliban come to be Formed?

People in Afghanistan who were Mujahideen, or Islamic guerilla fighters who had fought against the Soviet occupation of Afghanistan (1979-1989) formed the group in the early 1990s. The group was helped by the CIA and its Pakistani counterpart, the Inter-Services Intelligence directorate (ISI). People from the Pashtun tribe who had studied in Pakistani madrasas, or seminaries, joined them. Taliban is Pashto for "students". One-third of Afghanistan is made up of people from the Pashtun ethnic group, and they make up a large part of Afghanistan's south and east. The people who live in Pakistan's north and west are also a big part of this group.

During the first years after the Soviet Union came to an end, the movement gained a lot of support by promising to bring stability and the rule of law back to Afghanistan after four years of fighting between different groups of mujahideen. In November 1994, the Taliban came to Kandahar, a crime-ridden city in the south. By September 1996, they had taken over the capital, Kabul, from President Burhanuddin Rabbani, an ethnic Tajik who they thought was anti-Pashtun and corrupt. It was in that year that the Taliban made Afghanistan an Islamic emirate, with Mullah Mohammed Omar, a cleric and veteran of the anti-Soviet resistance, in charge as amir al-mu'minin, or "commander of the faithful", at the top. In 2001, a group of people overthrew the regime that had been in power for about 90 per cent of the country.

The Taliban used a harsh form of justice as they took over more and more land. Pre-Islamic tribal law and interpretations of the Sharia that were shaped by the strict Wahhabi beliefs of the madrasas' Saudi sponsors were used to make Taliban law. The Ministry for the Promotion of Virtue and Prevention of Vice demanded that women wear the chadri, or head-to-toe burqa, as well as a ban on music and TV, and jailed men whose beards it thought were too short.

How has the Rest of the World Responded to Them?

It's been more than two decades since governments and other international bodies joined forces with the US to get rid of the Taliban and improve Afghanistan's government, democratic institutions and civil society.

Armed force. Troops from the United States quickly took over Afghanistan in October 2001. They then launched an insurgency against the Afghan government that the United States helped set up in Afghanistan. The North Atlantic Treaty Organization (NATO), the world's most powerful security alliance, and three US administrations all tried to stop the group from fighting back during a war that killed more than 6,000 US troops and contractors and more than 1,100 NATO troops, but they failed. More than 47,000 civilians and an estimated 73,000 Afghan troops and police officers were killed from 2007 to 2021. Tens of thousands of Taliban fighters are also thought to have died in the fight against Afghanistan. In 2011, the number of US troops in Afghanistan reached about 100,000. In 2003, NATO took charge of foreign forces for the first time, making it the first time NATO had an operational commitment outside of Europe. At its peak, NATO had more than 130,000 troops from 50 different countries in Afghanistan, and they came from many different countries. In the 2020 US-Taliban agreement, the US said that if the Taliban kept their promises, they would have to leave Afghanistan with all of their troops. In August 2021, the United States finished taking all of its troops out of Afghanistan.

Sanctions. In 1999, the UN Security Council put sanctions on the regime because it kept Al Qaeda in the country. After 9/11, the sanctions got worse. They try to get money from Taliban leaders and stop them from going on most trips. There was also an arms embargo put on the Taliban by the Security Council. The United States and the European Union have added sanctions.

Democratic changes and help. Dozens of countries have helped Afghanistan, and 75 per cent of the government's expenses are paid for by grants from other countries, according to a report from the World Bank in 2019. However, many Western countries have stopped giving aid, and the World Bank has blocked the Taliban from getting millions of dollars after the group took over. This could cause even more economic problems.

Investigation. A group of people called the "Taliban" is now being investigated by the International Criminal Court for allegedly committing crimes against humanity and other abuses against Afghan civilians since 2003. The US and Afghan forces are also being investigated for possible war crimes, too.

When it comes to the Taliban's Money and Support from Other Countries, How is it Going?

Before they took over, the Taliban mostly made money through illegal activities like opium poppy cultivation, drug trafficking, extortion of local businesses, and kidnapping, says the UN monitoring group. Between $300 million and $1.6 billion is how much they make each year. People who grow opium poppy could make about $460 million in 2020, according to one report. They have also made extra money by illegally mining and getting money from other countries, even though the UN has strict rules about this. It's not clear how the Taliban will make money under the new government.

Many experts say that the Pakistani security establishment is still giving money and logistical support to the Taliban, as well as giving sanctuary to Taliban militants, in an effort to fight India's influence in Afghanistan. Islamabad doesn't believe these claims. A group called Tehrik-e-Taliban Pakistan has also been fighting in Pakistan. This group is not the same as the group in Afghanistan.

Do Afghans Like the Taliban?

For many years after they lost power, the Taliban had much support from people. Most Pashtuns and people who live in rural areas of Afghanistan have a lot of sympathy for armed groups like the Taliban. This is what the Asia Foundation, a US-based non-profit-making organisation, found in 2009. Some of the anger that led some Afghans to support the Taliban and other groups was because they didn't like public institutions.

This is different from when the same survey was done in 2019. Only 13.4 per cent of Afghans said they had a good feeling about the Taliban. It was important to protect women's rights, freedom of speech, and the current constitution in Afghanistan when peace talks broke down in early 2021. Around 44 per cent of Afghans who were asked said that they thought Afghanistan could be at peace in the next two years.

UN Refugee Agency. By the end of this year, more than half a million Afghans could have fled. In addition, a group of former officials, local militia members, and Afghan security forces called the National Resistance Front formed in the remote and mountainous Panjshir Province. They call themselves the National Resistance Front. After more than a week of fighting, the Taliban took control of the province. The resistance group has said that they will keep fighting against the Taliban.

The goal of this book is to look at Afghanistan's problems and challenges before and after the Taliban took over. I have learned a lot about this subject during my short time as an academician in this field. There have been many books written about Afghanistan, but each one talks about a different subject. I came up with the idea for this book when I realised that even though there are many books about Afghanistan, each one talks about a different subject. It will also look at several different issues and problems together in this book.

The book is meant to give an overview of Afghanistan's situation after the US forces left and the Taliban take over on August 15, 2021. This book takes a complete look at everything and explains it in detail. Every chapter has its own introduction that gives the reader a quick overview of the Taliban's influence in Afghanistan. The book is made up of 10 chapters that talk about different issues and problems. This book talks about Afghanistan's problems and challenges. Feminism, Peace and Afghanistan, why Afghanistan is considered to be a graveyard of empires, the Chinese desire to be in Afghanistan, the rights of women who are convulsed in Afghanistan, and the Panjshir resistance are also talked about.

As a whole, this book is an effort to give people an idea of what happened in Afghanistan before and after the Taliban took over. This book is meant for students, teachers, academics, and other professionals to use as a guide when they need help. The collection of articles will serve as a valuable resources tool for research and study as well as assist in the development of country India.

Neeraj Singh Manhas
Director of Research
Indo-Pacific, Raisina House
New Delhi

Acknowledgements

This book could not have been possible without the support of my well-wishers. I want to express my heartfelt gratitude to worthy Dr. Anurag Gangal, my teacher, Professor and Head of Department of Political Science, University of Jammu. Ms. Meenakshi Sambyal for being a source of inspiration, encouragement and providing me moral support. My thanks are also due to Associate Professor Dr. H. A. Mansuri, my supervisor, Department of Political Science, Sardar Patel University, for providing requisite help and constant support.

I would like to thanks Maj Gen (Dr.) Rajan Kochhar, VSM, for his innovative skills and providing me immense help in writing the Foreword for my book.

The journey of this book would not have been possible without the relentless support of my parents, the love of my sister Ms. Vanshika Manhas for exhibiting patience in all my endeavours throughout. This book is able to see the light of day with the divine blessings of my late grandparents.

Finally, I would like to thank KW Publishers for publishing and giving final shape to this book.

Neeraj Singh Manhas

Contributors

Shubhangi Misra is a Research Analyst at Intelligentsia Risk Advisors, New Delhi. She holds a Master's degree in International Relations from Queen Mary University of London. She has written several articles for a London-based online political platform covering varied subjects like India's vaccine diplomacy and the politics of gun reform in the US. She has previously volunteered at the Ministry of Social Justice and Empowerment, Government of India.

Anisha Maulida is an MPhil scholar and completed her Master's in Peace and Conflict Studies at the University of Oslo. She holds a Bachelor's degree in International Relations from Universitas Brawijaya, Indonesia. Her main research interests include violent extremism, terrorism, protest, nuclear and disarmament, and the dynamics of peace and conflict in MENA, South Asia, and Southeast Asia.

Tamanna Khosla is a Director of Prajna Initiative, USA. She has completed her Master's, MPhil and PhD in political theory from JNU, New Delhi. She has specialised in Multiculturalism, and Feminism. Most her articles are related to political philosophy international relations, sociology and comparative politics, feminism. She has taught in DU for several years.

Neeraj Singh Manhas is a Director, Indo-Pacific, Raisina House, New Delhi. Currently, he is a doctoral scholar in international relations at Sardar Patel University, Gujarat, India. He has previously completed his MPhil in Political Science. At present, he is visiting fellow at Anand Law College,

Gujarat, and a fellow at Global Policy, Diplomacy, and Sustainability (GPODS) Fellowship programme. He has participated in various national and international seminars and conferences, presented and published over a hundred papers.

Rajkumar Singh is Professor for the last 23 years and presently Head of the University Department of Political Science with Dean, Faculty of Social Sciences at the Bhupendra Narayan Mandal University, Madhepura (Bihar), India. In addition to 19 books published, there are about 900 articles to his credit in several national and international journals and daily newspapers. His most recent books are *Pandemic Covid-19: Major Effects and Side Effects* and *Social Justice and Reservation in Indian Polity.*

Jay Maniyar is a Researcher for the National Maritime Foundation (NMF), New Delhi, India. He is presently writing two books for the NMF on Japan and the Republic of Korea's (South Korea) geo-political, geo-economic, and geo-strategic interests in the Indian Ocean.

Suchita Sharma has completed Masters of Philosophy in Defence and Strategic Studies from University of Madras, Chennai. She holds Post-Graduate degree in Defence and Strategic Studies from Punjabi University, Patiala. She worked as a Lecturer in Defence Studies at F. C. College, Hisar (Haryana). Prior to that, she had been a Research Assistant in the Military Literature Festival Association, Chandigarh. She is an avid reader, writer and researcher. Her area of study includes Strategic and Security Studies in South Asia, India's neighbourhood, India's foreign and defence policies.

Puyesh Kant Sharma is an Assistant Professor in Political Science at the Department of Higher Education, University of Jammu. He has completed his doctoral thesis in International Studies from Jawaharlal Nehru University, New Delhi and MPhil and MA in Political Science from Jamia Millia Islamia, New Delhi. He has qualified UGC NET JRF in Political Science, presented several papers in national and international seminars and published several articles in edited books, newspapers and magazines.

Rekha Kumari R. Singh is currently an Associate Professor at Anand College of Legal Studies, and also I/C Principal of the College. She is also I/C Dean, Faculty of Law, Sardar Patel University, Gujarat.

Vibhaa Sreedhar is a final year law student at SASTRA Deemed University, Thanjavur, Tamil Nadu. She has a keen interest in international law, international relations and human rights.

1. Afghanistan's Modern Taliban Era: A Glass Half Full

Shubhangi Misra

Introduction

The past few years have witnessed a tremendous amount of focus on the Afghan region with regard to the hasty process of the American and NATO allied forces departing from the south-central Asian country and the dreaded return of the Taliban to power. Established in 1996 after seizing of Kabul under the leadership of Soviet veterans Mohammad Ghaus, Mullah Mohammad Omar, Mullah Hasan Omar, and Mullah Mohammad Abbas, the Taliban aimed at the restoration of peace after the Soviet invasion as well as the civil war, enforcement of the Sharia law, and overall protecting the virtue of the Islamic sanctity. The attack on the US on September 11, 2001, by the terrorist organisation Al-Qaeda which had sought refuge in the Taliban-run Afghanistan, jolted the US and the world alike, soon after which the former US President George Bush pledged to avenge the attacks by declaring a war on terror in the form of Operation Enduring Freedom. While the US government officials announced that terrorism has been eradicated in the country in December 2001, the constant attacks and resurgence of the Taliban in Afghanistan has been well documented in the last 20 years. Although it was vehemently believed that the death of Osama bin Laden, the head of the Al-Qaeda, in Abbottabad, Pakistan would significantly reduce the Taliban's impact on the region, it was too soon to predict the fate of Afghanistan, for things escalated thereafter, leading to the Doha Convention of February 2020. The Convention between the US and the Taliban saw the two agreeing upon the withdrawal of all foreign troops from Afghan soil and the Taliban's cooperation in ensuring that the Afghan soil is never used for terrorist endeavours, along with the release of prisoners of war on both sides.

This paper shall elucidate the current Taliban regime and its position in the modern world, as opposed to its stance in the 1990s and the early 2000s. Moreover, this paper shall also try and shed light on the ongoing developments in the region under the leadership of the current Taliban leaders, who have been conflicting and contradicting amongst themselves.

The Taliban and the 1990s

To understand the present scenario in Afghanistan, it is important to understand how it all began. The emergence of the Taliban in 1996 stemmed from its angst towards foreign invaders: both, the Soviets and the Americans. The adamant determination to establish an all-Islamic regime in Afghanistan drove the Taliban towards violence and incessant ruthlessness, which took shape in the form of assaulting women, decapitating petty criminals, and even murdering the former prime minister and other key players in Afghan politics. The Taliban's tremendous support towards militant organisations such as the Islamic State (IS) and the Al-Qaeda and the likes of them who were dedicated to the destruction and annihilation of the Western powers drew massive amounts of attention from the world, but it was never enough to declare a "war on terror", which subsequently happened after the September 11 attacks on US soil. The 9/11 attacks are known as the most devastating attacks on the US, which naturally alarmed the then US President who declared a war on terror—meaning a direct attack on the Al-Qaeda and the Taliban. Just a few weeks after the attack the US, along with its Allied North Atlantic Treaty Organisation (NATO) forces invaded Afghanistan and thus began a 20-year war—the longest and the most expensive war for the US, which cost the country over US$ 2.3 trillion over the span of two decades (*USA Today*, 2021).

What was it about the Taliban in the 1990s and early 2000s that caused turmoil in the region and the world? Their sheer hatred for the West, fused with ruthlessness against their "own" people was unequivocally worrisome in the field of international relations, geopolitics, and human rights.

The ideological perspective of the Taliban stems from a hard-core and extreme form of the Deobandi branch of Islam which has its roots in British-ruled India. As Kotokey and Borthakur (2021) mention, the intense following for the extreme Deobandi Islamism within the practitioners resulted in the creation of the strictest interpretation of the Sharia law which "eliminated the role of tribal and feudal structures, Khan and the role of Maliks, and completely debased the Deobandi tradition of learning and reform, and hence once they came to power in Afghanistan, they became fiercely opposed to modernism" (Kotokey and Borthakur, 2021). These Deobandi followers who were also the future leaders of the Taliban, aimed at transforming Afghanistan into a "pure Islamic Emirate", which also resulted in changing the official name of the country from Islamic State of Afghanistan to the Islamic Emirate of Afghanistan, which was also a means to revolt against the modern concept of democracy (Wani, 2021).

During their reign in the 1990s, well into the 2000s, the Taliban was notoriously infamous for imposing the harshest rules and regulations abiding by the Sharia law, which included public executions and amputations of criminals, banning women from leaving their houses without a male companion, and even beating women who were seen revolting against the laws. The extremist regime was also known for its massive strides in destroying monuments which were of cultural importance, such as the Bamiyan Buddha statue (MEI, 2012), as well as attacking infrastructure vital for Afghanistan as a country, such as the Afghan Parliament, to evidently portray their rejection of a democratic form of government in the country.

The initial defeat of the Taliban in 2001 at the hands of the Western coalition left the regime's members seeking asylum in both Pakistan and Baluchistan (Johnson, 2007); however, within two years Afghanistan's national security started to deteriorate again with the resurgence of the militant organisation (ibid.). The simultaneous war and invasion in Iraq had drastically reduced the attention of the US from Afghanistan, further compromising its security, with several intelligence, special forces and aviation assets diverted towards Iraq from Afghanistan (ibid.).

The Prolonged Process of Withdrawal

After ten years of war in Afghanistan in 2011 and the death of the infamous leader of Al-Qaeda, Osama bin Laden, further marked a significant move in the US' war against terror, following which talks of withdrawal from Afghanistan increased rapidly. Former President Barack Obama announced the plan to withdraw around 30,000 troops by 2012, while the rest of the troops were to remain until the US and the Taliban come to a solution during their preliminary peace talks. In 2014, Barack Obama outlined a timeline to withdraw a majority of the US forces from Afghanistan by 2016 in order to enable the Hamid Karzai government in Afghanistan to effectively take control over the country's national security.

With the election of Donald Trump as the President of the United States, Afghanistan witnessed the most powerful non-nuclear bomb on suspected self-proclaimed Islamic State militants in Nanagarhar province. (*New York Times*, 2017a). This incident triggered a series of strategic actions in response to the emergence of the Taliban and Islamic extremism, such as the deployment of adding several thousand troops to Helmand province (*New York Times*, 2017b).Throughout the next few years, the Taliban carried out several major attacks against Afghan civilians, killing dozens of people. These violent attacks only escalated the situation in the West, which resulted in the Trump administration cutting off security assistance to Pakistan worth billions of dollars amid Trump's serious accusations on the neighbouring country for harbouring Taliban militants and terrorists (*New York Times*, 2018).

By 2019, both the US and the Taliban began to concretely negotiate peace talks in Doha, revolving around the departure of the US and NATO troops from Afghanistan in return for the Taliban's guarantee to block international terrorist groups to operate from Afghan soil, as well as to ensure that no terrorist attacks are undertaken against the US and its allies (*New York Times*, 2019). On February 29, 2020, the US and the Taliban signed the significant agreement which formally announced the withdrawal of the Western troops by May 2021 (US Department of Defense, 2020). The troops finally began to be withdrawn from Afghan soil in 2020, and before the inauguration of President Joe Biden in January 2021, the Trump administration planned to halve the number of troops to 2,500 (ibid.). With the inauguration of President Biden, the newly established administration announced the postponement of the deadline to withdraw the troops from May 1, 2021, to September 11, 2021, regardless of the progress made in intra-Afghan peace talks (White House, 2021).

Have They Really Changed?

With the departure of the US and NATO allies during the months of July and August this year, the Taliban rapidly began to regain control of Afghanistan. Horrific, gut-wrenching images and videos of Afghans trying to flee their homes, with people suspended by the wings of aircraft immediately brought the world's undivided attention towards Afghanistan's depleting situation (Reuters, 2021a). The Western intelligence's claims of the fall of Afghanistan under the Taliban's regime within three to six months (Reuters, 2021b) were invalidated by August 2021, as the Afghan President Hamid Karzai absconded the country. The Taliban's swift invasion of the presidential palace marked the fall of Kabul, while foreign troops were still on Afghan soil. Although the militant organisation has consistently reiterated its plans to legitimise themselves as the sole administration of Afghanistan—by allowing women to pursue education, for instance—the Taliban has not been known to be a trustworthy entity. In 2007, Thomas Johnson stated "…it is clear that Afghanistan is anything but a stable and secure country. Indeed, the situation in Afghanistan has become extremely volatile." Fourteen years later the statement remains true to its core, with the Taliban's robust resurgence in the region and its subsequent and consistent violations of human rights on an unprecedented scale. With the departure of the foreign forces from the Afghan soil, the Taliban has oscillated its stance on human rights on the daily; the decision to allow women to pursue education, which was considered a milestone achievement, was soon eradicated as only girls aged under 12 are currently allowed to attend schools, and female students and employees at universities must wear hijabs. At the same time, members of the Taliban vandalised posters and images of women in public as a sign of their ideology. Moreover, the Taliban was responsible for a bomb attack at a school in May 2021, killing several students and teaching staff (Swails, 2021).

The Taliban has been consistent in contradicting its stances for the past two decades and ever since its takeover of Kabul in August 2021, the Taliban has conveyed mixed messages with regard to their approach in governing Afghanistan. After the attack outside the Hamid Karzai Airport in August 2021 by the Islamic State-Khorasan(IS-K), which killed over a hundred people as well as a dozen American soldiers, the Taliban offered to cooperate with the US in aiding assistance and security to their personnel during evacuation process (Gardner, 2021).

As Kotokey and Borthakur (2021) opine, "the ideological transition is mainly a part of the strategic discourse where aspirations to both inspire the insurgency and to become a legitimate authority in the country drive them to change their image which they feel was created by the Western powers."

Women in Afghanistan

Women and women's rights have been the centre of attention since the return of the Taliban which had been known to be compromised and brutally discarded in the past. The current Taliban regime initially permitted women and girls to attend schools and universities, a step that was definitely welcomed globally for it allowed a glimpse of hope for women in Taliban-ruled Afghanistan. During a recent interview with the *New York Times*, Zabihullah Mujahid, the official spokesperson for the Taliban, reiterated the regime's plan to establish a more tolerable administration as compared to that in the 1990s. This article, however, was published a day after the Taliban announced that women would be safest at homes "until more rank-and-file Taliban fighters have been trained in how not to mistreat them" (*New York Times*, 2021). The Taliban has also so far only permitted primary education to girls, resuming secondary education only for boys until a "secure transportation system" is in place for female students, while education for women at universities continues, although with a physical segregation between male and female students, along with mandatory hijabs for female employers and students at the universities (Robertson, 2021). At the same time, women have been completely excluded from administrative roles within the government (Robertson, 2021), a move that has reversed all the progress that was made within the last twenty years.

Role of the UN

During the 76th United Nations General Assembly in 2021, one of the most feared topics was the question of inclusion and representation of Afghanistan via the Taliban—something that the world had never hoped to witness. The Taliban persistently sought the approval of the UN as well as other world leaders, appointing their Doha-based spokesperson, Suhail Shaheen as the Afghanistan Ambassador to the UN (BBC, 2021a). The plea was ultimately rejected, announcing that Ghulam Isaczai shall remain the official Afghan ambassador to the UN (ibid.). Afghanistan's neighbours China and Pakistan are the only two countries so far that have accepted the Taliban as the country's legitimate ruler, with Pakistan's Prime Minister forwarding the agenda at the UN in the name of "conserving human rights" (UN, 2021), even though the Taliban have made it abundantly clear that public executions will be back in Afghanistan, commemorating their stance with the execution of four men accused of kidnapping (BBC, 2021b).

In addition to this, the UN has also pledged to aid the Taliban with US$ 1.2 billion to avert the humanitarian crisis in Afghanistan (US News, 2021). Raising money for a terrorist organisation that is currently the governing body of a country in the name of human rights seems inexplicable, and more so feels like a step closer for the Taliban to be legitimised by the West.

The Taliban vs IS-K Rift

The Islamic State Khorasan was formally established in 2015 as an offshoot of the Islamic State of Iraq and Syria (ISIS), which majorly consists of former members of the Taliban in Afghanistan and the Tehrik-e Taliban in Pakistan (Ibrahimi and Akbarzadeh, 2019). The IS-K has maintained a controversial relationship with the Taliban in Afghanistan, wavering from a supporter to a competition from time to time. More often than not, the IS-K has been competing against the Taliban in mobilising the masses towards it, including persuading the Taliban fighters to defect to the IS-K, with the promise of a more radical and a "more Islamic" movement and questioning the jihadist agendas of the Taliban (Ibrahimi and Akbarzadeh, 2019). The IS-K has also recently sought cooperation from regional partners such as Pakistan in the name of jihad, while also significantly gaining support and attracting resources from ISIS supporters worldwide (ibid.).

As Ibrahimi and Akbarzadeh state, "IS-K's trans-nationalist rhetoric and more explicit sectarian agenda has indirectly benefited the Taliban by posing a threat that is seen as more urgent than the Taliban insurgency by the Afghan government, the United States, and North Atlantic Treaty Organization (NATO) forces and other countries in the region" (2019).

The IS-K has gained momentum in the recent years through its constant attacks on civilian targets, especially Shia Hazara mosques, protests, as well as educational centres, especially those educating female students. The Taliban and the IS-K and their engagement in violent conflicts in the region has been a topic of discussion for scholars worldwide to understand the "dynamics of conflict of cooperation between various jihadist groups" (ibid.).

Ever since the Taliban's takeover of Kabul in August 2021, the IS-K has consistently been attacking civilians so as to undermine the Taliban's position. The Taliban was seen keeping its end of the promise from the Doha Convention to eradicate terrorist activities from Afghanistan after the chaotic, massively disruptive, and deadly attack at the Hamid Karzai Airport in August 2021 by the IS-K which killed over a hundred people who were trying to flee Afghanistan. The Taliban offered to assist the US personnel in providing a security perimeter for a safe withdrawal of the troops. In addition to this, the Taliban avenged the deaths of several people outside a mosque in Kabul that was attacked by the IS-K, with the destruction of the terrorist group's cell in the capital city, killing all the IS members present inside (*Hindustan Times*, 2021).

These recent anecdotes point towards a Taliban that is so far more intolerant rather than supportive of militant organisations such as the

IS-K which pose a threat to not only Afghanistan, but also grasps the attention of world players, including neighbouring countries like India.

Conclusion

The current situation in Afghanistan remains uncertain and only makes one wonder as to how long it would take for the world, and the world leaders to unwillingly accept the Taliban—literally the largest militant organisation—as a country's legitimate governing administration. The regime's constant conflicts with regional factions such as the IS-K, along with the absence of a framework to secure human rights especially for women, have hindered the process of its legitimisation on the global stage. Afghanistan's geopolitical significance to its neighbours such as China, India, and Pakistan are well known to the world, while the Western powers understand its vitality as both a link between Asia, Central Asia, and Europe, as well as a safe haven for terrorism which poses a greater risk of terrorism than ever. With the advancement in technologies and means to attract resources from across the world, jihadist groups such as the IS-K, Al-Qaeda, Tehrik-e Taliban, and other regional militant organisations have successfully gained momentum in the past few years. Moreover, along with the exit of foreign powers and their extensively equipped military personnel and intelligence, these militant organisations hold much more power than they did some twenty years ago. The Taliban's dire need for acceptance from the world might move towards actually resolving the problem of terrorism in the region, however its own personal vendetta to purify Afghanistan into its true Islamic state has left everyone in anticipation, for it is too soon to concretely analyse the future of Afghanistan.

References

BBC News. (2021a). "Taliban ask to speak at UN General Assembly in New York". https://www.bbc.com/news/world-asia-58632147

BBC News. (2021b). "Afghanistan: Executions will return, says senior Taliban official". https://www.bbc.com/news/world-asia-58675153

Brown University, Watson Institute. (2021). "U.S. Budgetary Costs of Post-9/11 Wars Through FY2022: $8 Trillion | Figures | Costs of War". https://watson.brown.edu/costsofwar/figures/2021/BudgetaryCosts

Centlivres, P. (2012). "The Death of the Buddhas of Bamiyan". https://www.mei.edu/publications/death-buddhas-bamiyan

Gardner, F. (2021). "Afghanistan airport attack: Who are IS-K?". BBC. https://www.bbc.com/news/world-asia-58333533

Hindustan Times. (2021). "Hours after Kabul mosque blast, Taliban destroy IS cell in Afghan capital". https://www.hindustantimes.com/world-news/hours-after-kabul-mosque-blast-taliban-destroy-is-cell-in-afghan-capital-101633341646413.html

Ibrahimi, N., and S. Akbarzadeh. (2019). "Intra-Jihadist Conflict and Cooperation: Islamic State–Khorasan Province and the Taliban in Afghanistan". *Studies in Conflict & Terrorism*, 43(12), 1086–1107. https://doi.org/10.1080/1057610x.2018.1529367

Johnson, T. (2007). "On the Edge of the Big Muddy: The Taliban Resurgence in Afghanistan". *China and Eurasia Forum Quarterly*, 5(2), pp. 93-129. https://apps.dtic.mil/sti/pdfs/ADA484262.pdf

Kotokey, A., and A. Borthakur. (2021). "The Ideological Trajectory within the Taliban Movement in Afghanistan". *Asian Journal of Middle Eastern and Islamic Studies*, 15(2), pp. 205-19.

Mashal, M. (2019). "Taliban Deputy Chief Arrives in Qatar for Talks with U.S.". *The New York Times*. https://www.nytimes.com/2019/02/24/world/asia/taliban-negotiator-afghanistan-qatar-us.html?module=inline

Reuters. (2021a). "Chaos, desperation at Kabul airport as Biden defends withdrawal from Afghanistan". https://www.reuters.com/world/asia-pacific/talibans-rapid-advance-across-afghanistan-2021-08-10/

Reuters. (2021b). "Taliban could take Afghan capital within 90 days after rapid gains—U.S. intelligence". https://www.reuters.com/world/asia-pacific/taliban-fighters-capture-eighth-provincial-capital-six-days-2021-08-11/

Robertson, N. (2021). "Taliban deny claims girls will be banned from school—but don't say when they'll be allowed in". CNN. https://edition.cnn.com/2021/09/18/asia/afghanistan-schools-girls-taliban-intl/index.html

Swails, B. (2021). "Women in Kabul return to work, school, and the streets, in defiance of the Taliban". CNN. https://edition.cnn.com/2021/10/04/asia/kabul-women-work-school-defiance-taliban-intl/index.html

Shesgreen, D. (2021). "'War rarely goes as planned': New report tallies trillions US spent in Afghanistan, Iraq". *USA Today*. https://eu.usatoday.com/story/news/politics/2021/09/01/how-much-did-war-afghanistan-cost-how-many-people-died/5669656001/

The New York Times. (2017a). "U.S. Drops 'Mother of All Bombs' on ISIS Caves in Afghanistan". https://www.nytimes.com/2017/04/13/world/asia/moab-mother-of-all-bombs-afghanistan.html?_r=0

The New York Times. (2017b). "Back in Afghan Hot Spot, U.S. Marines Chase Diminished Goal". https://www.nytimes.com/2017/07/14/world/asia/back-in-afghan-hot-spot-us-marines-chase-diminished-goals.html

The New York Times. (2018). "Cutting Off Pakistan, U.S. Takes Gamble in Complex Afghan War". https://www.nytimes.com/2018/01/05/world/asia/pakistan-aid-afghan-war.html

The New York Times. (2021). "The Taliban wants to forget the past, a leader tells *The Times*, but there will be some restrictions". https://www.nytimes.com/2021/08/25/world/asia/taliban-spokesman-interview.html

The U.S. Department of State. (2020). "Agreement for Bringing Peace to Afghanistan between the Islamic Emirate of Afghanistan which is not recognized by the United States as a state and is known as the Taliban and the United States of America". https://www.state.gov/wp-content/uploads/2020/02/Agreement-For-Bringing-Peace-to-Afghanistan-02.29.20.pdf

The White House. (2021). "Remarks by President Biden on the Way Forward in Afghanistan". https://www.whitehouse.gov/briefing-room/speeches-remarks/2021/04/14/remarks-by-president-biden-on-the-way-forward-in-afghanistan/

United Nations. (2021). "Pakistan—Prime Minister Addresses United Nations General Debate", 76th Session (English). [video] https://www.youtube.com/watch?v=2qUryNMzrdw

US News. (2021). "Donors Pledge $1.2 Billion in Emergency Funds for Afghans". https://www.usnews.com/news/world/articles/2021-09-13/un-seeks-606-million-for-afghanistan-after-taliban-takeover

Wani, Z. A. (2021). "Afghanistan's Neo-Taliban Puzzle". *South Asia Research*, 41(2), 220–37. https://doi.org/10.1177/02627280211000165

2. The Impact of the US Withdrawal from Afghanistan: Pakistan and China

Anisha Maulida

Introduction

This summer, the United States has finally ended America's longest war in Afghanistan which was marked by the withdrawal of all their military forces on August 30, 2021 (Zucchino, 2021). This withdrawal is a testament to America's failure to implement its counterinsurgency strategy, which in turn provides opportunities for the terrorist group, the Taliban, to regain control of Afghanistan.

As in 2017, the number of the US military troops had diminished with 11,000 US troops reportedly in Afghanistan (Thomas, 2021). Under Trump's administration, he set to limit additional troops to around 3,500 and by the end of 2017, the total number of US troops deployed in Afghanistan was between 14,000 and 15,000 (Thomas, 2021). However, by mid-2019, Trump expressed his frustration with the lack of progress of the US military against the Taliban and promised to leave Afghanistan as soon as possible. On February 29, 2020, Trump made an agreement with the Taliban in Doha to subsequently pull out all the foreign forces, including the US troops from Afghan soil (Anonymous, 2020). Before the elected US president, Joe Biden, took the White House, the US had reduced its military to 2,500 troops; meanwhile, the NATO European troops were about 5,000, hence, the total number of active militaries in Afghan soil was 7,500; the Trump White House pledged to leave the country by May 1 (Filkins, 2021).

Moreover, as Biden took office, Trump left him with just two options: (1) send back thousands of US troops to Afghanistan for nothing but endless war, or (2) to completely withdraw from Afghanistan (Tucker, 2021). Considering the fruitless mission in Afghanistan, the high cost of war, and the growing opinion of the American public to end the war urged Biden to completely leave Afghanistan and quickly withdraw all the remaining troops in the country. Most of the US troops had left in July and to end violence on civilians, the Afghan official government offered a "power-sharing" with the Taliban (BBC, 2021). As a consequence, the Taliban made a huge gain on August 16, in which 391 districts fell under Taliban control (BBC, 2021).

Fig 1: Afghanistan Map in July vs August

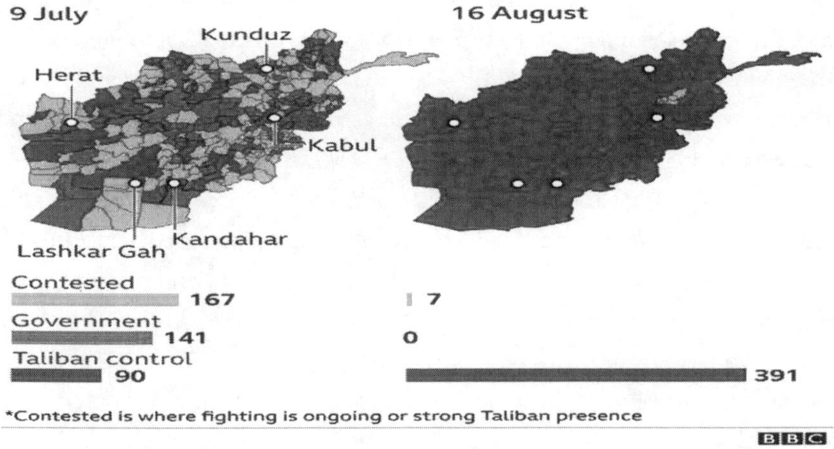

Source: BBC Research. Districts according to 2005 government boundaries.

The Taliban takeover caused thousands of Afghans to flee the country to seek asylum or another pathway to safely migrate abroad (HRW, 2021). Although the Taliban had pledged to protect the civilians and support human rights, including women and girls, media freedom, and protection for former government personnel, many Afghans still fear persecution or reprisals under Taliban rule (HRW, 2021). However, Afghanistan will not suffer alone. The US withdrawal followed by the Taliban's seizure of power in Afghanistan could further trigger the instability of regional peace and security and become a new challenge for the economy of its neighbouring countries, especially Pakistan and China, that have interests in Afghanistan. This chapter will further delve into a general discussion of the positive and negative implication of the US withdrawal from Afghanistan to Pakistan and China, who gains what and how.

Pakistan and China Relations to Afghanistan

Pakistan-Afghanistan Turbulent Relations

As a Muslim country, Pakistan has always promoted closer cooperation and relationship with other Muslim countries, yet this is not the case with Afghanistan. Afghanistan has a hostile attitude as a neighbour and acted negatively, other than the binding role the Muslim faith was expected to play, in which Pakistan has to live with it (Durani and Khan, 2009, p. 27). The history of tense relations of Pakistan and Afghanistan triggered by five issues: sovereignty, security, geopolitical dynamics, cross-border ties, and connectivity and trade (Threlkeld and Easterly, 2021).

In 1947, after the establishment of Pakistan, Pakistan-Afghanistan relations were characterised by first, *border disputes*, particularly Durand Line, where Afghanistan did not recognise the Durand Line as a legitimate international border (Durani and Khan, 2009, p. 29). This caused the two countries concern about the violation of *sovereignty*. Pakistan's sovereignty concern rose as Afghanistan supported and provided assistance to pro-Pashtunistan. As a matter of fact, many Afghan officials backed the creation of a confederation to include Afghanistan, Pakistan, and Pashtunistan (Threlkeld and Easterly, 2021). Meanwhile, Afghanistan worried about Pashtun sovereignty due to the fact that the policy of abolishing provincial boundaries policy effectively incorporated the Federally Administrated Tribal Areas (FATA) into Pakistan's territory and negated its autonomous status (Threlkeld and Easterly, 2021). Third, *bilateral* and *trade agreement* between Pakistan and Afghanistan restored, as both parties managed to reconcile on Tehran Accord in 1963 and reach an agreement on Durand Line in the 1970s (Durani and Khan, 2009). Both sides to reopen their closed borders and resume trade and commercial ties which was a sigh of relief for Afghanistan's economy (Durani and Khan, 2009). However, during the Cold War era, both states were rivals in the geopolitical divide.

The blame game continued post 9/11 in 2001. Cross-border issues continue until today, May 2007 as an example, when eight Pakistani soldiers reportedly died as the Afghan soldiers entered Pakistan and attacked military posts (Siddique, 2011). Both states accused each other of fomenting their insurgencies. Moreover, the relationship between the two states pivot on the topic of Pashtun population and the Taliban. With these two issues, Pakistan's policy towards Afghanistan has always utilised these to assert strategic relations with Afghanistan (Siddique, 2011). Despite the accusation of providing safe haven to the terrorist groups, Al-Qaeda, and supporting the Taliban, Pakistan agreed to assist the US in counterterrorist missions. Pakistan moved 100,000 troops to its western border to target the militants (Siddique, 2011). Today, as the US military troops have left the country, Pakistan could do nothing but support the Afghanistan government under the Taliban. In order to gain its strategic interest, Pakistan aimed to maintain its relations with Afghanistan which could be seen through its actions towards Afghanistan.

China-Afghanistan Relations

Unlike Pakistan, in the relations between China and Afghanistan, China is rather more careful in maintaining good relations with Kabul. Beijing has long been concerned about the spread of extremist ideas to its Westernmost territory, Xinjiang. The tensions have been particularly about ethnic unrest and terrorism in Xinjiang. The Sunni Uyghur militant groups that are based on the border of Pakistan-Afghanistan have claimed responsibility for a small number of attacks in China (Kley, 2014).

Therefore, China has envisaged a stable situation in Afghanistan as it is important for Chinese interests. After 9/11 tragedy, China has made a minimal contribution to Afghanistan with a very modest reconstruction aid of US$ 250 million (Kley, 2014). China has been completely on the sideline and took a low-key diplomatic approach—delegate someone to read out statements in the meetings (Kley, 2014). However, the two states' relations have advanced since 2012 when the security chief, Zhou Yongkang, visited Kabul, the most senior Chinese leader to visit the country in decades (Kley, 2014). China further appointed a special envoy to Afghanistan in 2014 and committed to develop its economic footprint in the country. On the other hand, the NATO withdrawal in 2014 indirectly affected China's western region security as the Afghan Taliban are sympathetic towards Uyghurs which could lead to several threats, including trafficking of personnel and weapons into Xinjiang, the spread of extremist ideology, and closer cooperation with terror organisations (Kley, 2014).

China's policy towards Afghanistan would remain to be diplomatic and economic engagement. China is likely to avoid military intervention in Afghanistan, and considering the tension in Xinjiang, Beijing fears that military intervention would invite trouble to China (Kley, 2014). One option of security cooperation would be providing a training or equipment for Afghanistan's security forces. Today, the security situation in Afghanistan is heating up again after the US and its allies withdraw from the country. The nature of Beijing-Kabul relationship would likely be twofold. First, fostering the economic partnership as Afghanistan's economy deteriorates after the US invasion, and second, maintaining the threat by non-interference in the other's internal affairs.

How Pakistan and China See the Taliban's Victory

Pakistan and Taliban

The emergence of the Taliban in 1996 ushered in close and friendly relations between Pakistan and Afghanistan than before (Threlkeld and Easterly, 2021). It was the first time that Pakistan had a relationship with the Afghan government that had no ties with India (Durani and Khan, 2009). As a matter of fact, Pakistan extended full diplomatic and economic support to Afghanistan under the Taliban government and accorded Taliban with diplomatic recognition in 1997 (Durani and Khan, 2009). Pakistan's full support to the Taliban government coincided with geo-economic and geostrategic considerations, such as securing a trade route to the landlocked countries in Central Asia, facilitating Kashmiri Mujahideen in training for freedom from India, and ending the civil war in Afghanistan that had chances to spill over to Pakistan's territories (Durani and Khan, 2009).

The friendly relationship between Taliban and Pakistan has changed after 9/11 as Pakistan distanced itself from the Taliban and yet, Pakistan allegedly continued to provide the group covert assistance and safe haven (Threlkeld and Easterly, 2021). Nonetheless, Islamabad has shown its proactive role in the region by facilitating meetings between the Taliban and Afghan officials along with the third party. Further, Pakistani intelligence has allegedly tortured the commanders of the Taliban. A commander who has been released revealed that he was mistreated and considered Pakistan as the main foe of the Taliban, Afghans, and the Islamic movement (Yousafzai, 2017). In addition to that, Pakistan Army chief, General Qamer Javed Bajwa, is more concerned about the Taliban's potential to destabilise Pakistan (Miller, 2021).

How, then, did the Pakistani government see the Taliban's victory in Afghanistan? What does the victory mean for Pakistan? Pakistan has suffered over the past years at the hands of Islamist terror groups launching attacks across the border from Afghanistan (Landale, 2021). Nonetheless, Pakistan needs to maintain its relationship with its close neighbour regardless of who is the ruler. The Prime Minister of Pakistan, Imran Khan, said that the world should give a chance to the Islamists and give them more time before judging their record on human rights (Findlay, 2021). Thus, the Taliban's victory is such a coin with two faces for Pakistan. On the one side, this could be a strategic win for Pakistan, and on the other hand, it will be a new challenge for Pakistan. I will further elaborate on this in the next section.

China and the Taliban

Perhaps, China's relationship with the Taliban is not as strong as Pakistan's. As China is not directly involved in the Afghanistan conflict, their relationship with the Taliban is tricky. It is important to note that China did not recognise the Taliban when the group first ruled Afghanistan in 1996 to 2001 (Grossman, 2021). However, the case is different this time—China seems willing to leverage its relations with the group. How will China deal with the group? It will not be a big problem for the Chinese government to deal with the Taliban because unlike the United States and Russia that has fought with Afghanistan, China's role in Afghanistan in the past years could be as a leverage at this point.

Prior to the Taliban's victory in Afghanistan, Beijing had started deepening diplomatic ties with the group and expressed their respect to the rights of the people of Afghanistan to decide their future (Johnson, 2021). This notion implies that the Taliban's victory reflects the people's will. China, furthermore, has predicted and been preparing for the possibility of the Taliban to resume its power in Afghanistan (Ng, 2021). For many years, China has been hedging their bets on the Taliban's victory by maintaining their communication with the group. For example, in 2018, China together with Pakistan had been engaged in a dialogue with the Taliban to discuss regional security and stability within Afghanistan (Azad, 2020).

However, China is concerned about their internal security because there is a possibility of the emergence of Islamist terrorist groups in China which are backed by the Afghan-based terrorist groups. Therefore, China supported the Taliban to be included in the Afghan government and, as an exchange for that, the Taliban obliged by not providing the Uyghur secessionist groups safe haven in Afghanistan and preventing them from crossing the border (Azad, 2020). Moreover, in order for the new Afghan interim government to revive Afghanistan's economy, the Taliban needs financial assistance from foreign countries to help them, particularly in reconstruction. With that, the Taliban will likely welcome infrastructure and investment projects in post-war Afghanistan. In addition, the Taliban spokesman, Suhail Shaheen, reiterated their support for Chinese investment in Afghanistan and to see China as a friend (India, 2021).

Big Wins and Lose Big

Let us delve into a discussion of the impacts of the US withdrawal from Afghanistan to Pakistan and China in this section. In the beginning, I have emphasised on bilateral relations between Afghanistan and Pakistan/

China and how both countries perceived the Taliban new government in Afghanistan. These all need to be taken into account before one could discuss the implication of the US decision to pull out their troops from the country. Particularly so because the US withdrawal has led the Taliban to seize power and dismiss the "official" Afghan government. Therefore, this chapter previously analysed how close is the relationship of both Pakistan and China to Afghanistan (under its official government), as well as how is the relationship of Pakistan and China with the Taliban then and now, along with the issues that both countries have with either the Afghan government or the Taliban.

Pakistan

After the US left Afghanistan and the Taliban seized power, Pakistan gained a strategic victory. First, pro-Islamabad government in Afghanistan. As I have previously mentioned, Islamabad had a rocky relationship with Kabul when the Taliban ruled the first time. Now, after 20 years, Pakistan will likely have more "friendly" bilateral relations with Afghanistan again and this is not a small matter. Second, India is the common enemy. Afghanistan's government had close ties with India which is Pakistan's foe. Meanwhile, the Taliban has no ties with India and India itself refused to deal with the groups and would continue to support opposition groups that are resisting the militants (Lawler, 2021). In this sense, one could project that Afghanistan under the Taliban administration would incline to Pakistan instead of India.

Third, trade cooperation. Despite the fact that Afghanistan and Pakistan are significant trading partners, Central Asia is also an important trading partner for Pakistan. Pakistan has a trade agreement with Uzbekistan, a country that is highly reliant on the Iranian seaport of Bandar Abbas accessed through Turkmenistan; however, they also had an agreement with Afghanistan for trade transit (Bhutta, 2021). This is good news for Pakistan as they also had Afghanistan-Pakistan Transit Trade Agreement (APTTA). Hence, with the good relationship the Pakistani government has with the Taliban in Afghanistan, this would be easier for Pakistan trading activities with Central Asia. Moreover, the APTTA gave access to Pakistan's trade with Central Asia for taking goods up to the border crossing points of Afghanistan with Uzbekistan, Tajikistan, and Turkmenistan (Bhutta, 2021). It is, therefore, through economic engagement between Pakistan and Afghanistan that it would create a positive dynamic on bilateral relations between the two states.

Fourth, a common belief that there is a likelihood that the US would outsource Afghanistan to Pakistan, hence it would open an opportunity to political engagement and economic incentives between the US and Pakistan (Sakhi and Pforzheimer, 2021). Last but not least, security and anti-terror cooperation—this one would be quite problematic. This last point would also be a loss for Pakistan because, in terms of security, it is not only regarding the regional borders, but also Pakistan's domestic security. The victory of the Taliban has emboldened regional Islamist militant groups, including the resurgence of Tehrik-e Taliban (TTP) or the Pakistani Taliban. However, both parties had discussed bilateral security cooperation, including measures needed at border crossings to stem the movement of terrorists into Pakistan (Gul, 2021). The Taliban also emphasised that no one will be allowed to use Afghan soil against Pakistan, hence the group will not let Afghanistan be a safe haven for the TTP and support Pakistan on this matter. Although, the TTP attacks have continued against Pakistani forces (Gul, 2021).

Moreover, it leads us to another negative impact of the US withdrawal to Pakistan. In terms of security, illicit drugs trafficking would also be a problem. Most of the money to fund the terrorist organisations in Pakistan and Afghanistan comes from narcotics trading, especially heroin, which has been done by the Taliban (Samad, 2014). Lastly, as the Taliban took control of the country, many Afghans fled to seek asylum, and many of them fled to Pakistan. It further created a refugee crisis in Pakistan in which they must allocate significant bandwidth, ensure adequate resources to registering and supporting the Afghan refugees as well as to take care of them.

China

One thing that could be highlighted from the US withdrawal from Afghanistan for China is that China has lost the influence of its biggest rival in the region; perhaps that is a relief for their government. Therefore, their relationship with the Taliban could show the US that China is the key player in the region, not the US. That is a win for China geopolitically. As what has been mentioned earlier, the impact on China will be two-fold. First let us begin from its mercantile interest in Afghanistan that would probably be a win for China.

In terms of economic cooperation, both Afghanistan and China at this point need each other. China is seeking business ventures inside Afghanistan and the Taliban, as has been mentioned, is likely to welcome and support the Chinese government. This is particularly because of the Afghan economic crisis, hence they need investors who can bring revenues to Afghanistan. However, it is interesting to note that Afghanistan is an insignificant market for China and there has been a limited number of projects in the country (Johnson, 2021).

Despite Afghanistan's vast mineral riches and optimism of extending the massive Chinese project of its Belt and Road Initiative (BRI), Afghanistan appears far from ready to serve as a link in that chain (Moritsugu, 2021). The reason for this could be the incomplete BRI project in a "stable" country and China is unable to secure the ongoing project in Pakistan (China-Pakistan Economic Corridor). With that in mind, one could imagine if the major BRI project took place in Afghanistan, which is notably still unstable for a such "mega project"—then, why put BRI at risk? Furthermore, there are two of China's projects that have not unlocked in Afghanistan. First, Mes Aynak copper mine project in 2008 which amounted to US$ 3 billion, and second, another Chinese company won the right to develop an oil field in Amu Darya in 2011.

If it is not for an economic interest, then what does China really seek from Afghanistan under the Taliban administration? Security and political interest. Both the Taliban and China have issues in human rights abuses, thus their bilateral relations would start from the *non-interference principle* that both parties agree to (Johnson, 2021). Both states will not intervene in the domestic affairs of the other. It implies that the Taliban cannot spread out extremism into China's controversial region, Xinjiang, that shares a border with Afghanistan, nor condemn the Chinese government's abuse to human rights against Uyghur Muslims. In exchange for this, the Chinese government cannot also condemn nor question the human rights violation that have been committed by the group, unless Chinese citizens are involved. This could wipe out the fear of Chinese government of the spillover effect of the rise of the Taliban in Afghanistan to its westernmost region, and halt the emergence of Islamist groups. Similar to their pledge to Pakistan, the Taliban will not allow the use of Afghan soil by the extremist groups to hold their training and exercise, meaning that Afghanistan is not a safe haven for the terrorist groups.

Conclusion

The US withdrawal from Afghan soil was put in consideration under Trump's administration since mid-2019 and, in 2020, an agreement was arrived at between the US and the Taliban, which stated that the US and its allies will pull out all military troops from Afghanistan. This compromise between the US and the Taliban depends on Biden as he took oath to the White House in 2021. Biden, then, decided to leave Afghanistan and withdraw all US military from Afghan soil. Such action has proven that the 20-year-war in Afghanistan was a failed US counterinsurgency strategy and, in fact, granted the Taliban control of the country again.

Pakistan and China, as the regional key players that border with Afghanistan, are clearly affected by these circumstances. For Pakistan, it is mostly a strategic victory rather than just sharing pain with Afghanistan. However, as for China, a strategic political and security cooperation should be built to foster their bilateral relations not only with Afghanistan as a country but the Taliban, as a terrorist group. Going forward, hedging strategy with the necessary evil (the Taliban) is crucial for both Pakistan and China to maintain the bilateral relationships, regional stability, and to build strong cooperation in future.

References

Anonymous. (2020, February 29). "Agreement for Bringing Peace to Afghanistan between the Islamic Emirate of Afghanistan which is not Recognized by the United States as a state and is known as the Taliban and the United States of America".

Retrieved from US Department of State. https://www.state.gov/wp-content/uploads/2020/02/Agreement-For-Bringing-Peace-to-Afghanistan-02.29.20.pdf

Azad, S. (2020, September 22). "China's Stake in the Afghan Peace Process". Retrieved from *The Diplomat*. https://thediplomat.com/2020/09/chinas-stake-in-the-afghan-peace-process/

BBC. (2021, August 16). "Mapping the Advance of the Taliban in Afghanistan". Retrieved from BBC. https://www.bbc.com/news/world-asia-57933979

Bhutta, Z. (2021, July 14). "Uzbekistan to use Pakistani seaports for trade". Retrieved from *The Express Tribune*. https://tribune.com.pk/story/2310371/uzbekistan-to-use-pakistani-seaports-for-trade

Durani, M. U., and A. Khan. (2009). "Pakistan-Afghan Relations: Historic Mirror". *The Dialogue*, IV(1), 25-64.

Filkins, D. (2021, March 4). "Trump's Deal to End War in Afghanistan Leaves Biden with 'A Terrible Situation'". (T. Gross, Interviewer)

Findlay, S. (2021, September 30). "'A win for Pakistan': Imran Khan gambles on Taliban ties". Retrieved from *Financial Times*. https://www.ft.com/content/257853d9-acb6-432b-92d4-a1b45335a388

Gul, A. (2021, September 6). "Afghan Taliban, Pakistan Discuss Anti-Terror Cooperation". Retrieved from VOA News. https://www.voanews.com/a/south-central-asia_afghan-taliban-pakistan-discuss-anti-terror-cooperation/6219314.html

Grossman, D. (2021, August 27). "Chinese Recognition of the Taliban Is All but Inevitable". Retrieved from RAND Corporation. https://www.rand.org/blog/2021/08/chinese-recognition-of-the-taliban-is-all-but-inevitable.html

HRW. (2021, September 9). "What's Next for Afghans Fleeing the Taliban?". Retrieved from *Human Rights Watch*. https://www.hrw.org/news/2021/09/09/whats-next-afghans-fleeing-taliban

India, P.T. (2021, July 10). "Taliban Says It Sees China as a 'Friend' of Afghanistan: Report". Retrieved from NDTV. https://www.ndtv.com/world-news/taliban-says-it-sees-china-as-a-friend-of-afghanistan-report-2483783

Johnson, I. (2021, August 24). "How Will China Deal With the Taliban?". Retrieved from Council on Foreign Relations. https://www.cfr.org/in-brief/china-afghanistan-deal-with-taliban

Kley, D. V. (2014). "China's Foreign Policy in Afghanistan". Lowy Institute.

Landale, J. (2021, September 3). "Afghanistan: What Rise of Taliban Means for Pakistan". Retrieved from BBC News. https://www.bbc.com/news/world-asia-58443839

Lawler, D. (2021, September 5). "What the Taliban victory means for Afghanistan's neighbors". Retrieved from AXIOS. https://www.axios.com/afghansitan-neighbors-relations-taliban-china-14e285a4-55f7-4b57-9c19-816a5fe1ee5b.html

Miller, M. C. (2021, August 25). "Pakistan's Support for the Taliban: What to Know". Retrieved from Council on Foreign Relations. https://www.cfr.org/article/pakistans-support-taliban-what-know

Moritsugu, K. (2021, August 23). "Risk and instability: Afghanistan seen as weak link for China's Belt and Road Initiative". Retrieved from *The Sydney Morning Herald*. https://www.smh.com.au/world/middle-east/risk-and-instablity-afghanistan-seen-as-weak-link-for-china-s-belt-and-road-initiative-20210823-p58kzh.html

Ng, A. (2021, August 23). "'Hedging their bets': Political experts weigh in on China's growing relations with the Taliban". Retrieved from CNBC News. https://www.cnbc.com/2021/08/23/china-and-taliban-relations-with-afghanistan-are-tricky-analysts-say.html

Sakhi, N., and A. Pforzheimer. (2021, July 29). "Missing the bigger implications of US withdrawal from Afghanistan". Retrieved from Middle East Institute. https://www.mei.edu

Samad, Y. (2014, March 10). "Understanding the Insurgency in Balochistan". *Commonwealth & Comparative Politics*, pp. 293-320.

Siddique, Q. (2011). "Pakistan's Future Policy Towards Afghanistan: A Look At Strategic Depth, Militant Movements and the Role of India and the US". Cophenhagen: Danish Institute for International Studies (DIIS).

Thomas, C. (2021). "U.S. Military Withdrawal and Taliban Takeover in Afghanistan: Frequently Asked Questions". Congressional Research Service.

Threlkeld, E., and G. Easterly. (2021). "Afghanistan-Pakistan Ties and Future Stability in Afghanistan". United States Institute of Peace.

Tucker, P. (2021, August 18). "Trump's Pledge to Exit Afghanistan Was a Ruse, His Final SecDef Says". Retrieved from *Defense One*. https://www.defenseone.com/policy/2021/08/trumps-pledge-exit-afghanistan-was-ruse-his-final-secdef-says/184660/

Yousafzai, S. (2017, July 12). "Taliban Commanders Say They Were Tortured by Pakistani Intelligence". Retrieved from *Daily Beast*. https://www.thedailybeast.com/taliban-commanders-say-they-were-tortured-by-pakistani-intelligence

Zucchino, D. (2021, September 22). "The U.S War in Afghanistan: How It Started, and How It Ended". Retrieved from *The New York Times*. https://www.nytimes.com/article/afghanistan-war-us.html

3. Feminism, Peace and Afghanistan: An Indian Feminist Perspective

Tamanna Khosla

A Brief Background

Afghanistan opened 2019 with robust talks of peace, which now dominated headlines about the country. However, we must look at history to avoid the repetition of past mistakes, which undermine human rights principles, especially human rights. The images and realities of repressed Afghan women hidden beneath their blue burqas shocked not only the international community but was used to help justify the 2001 US-led intervention in Afghanistan. Yet, the current peace negotiation being brokered seems to have forgotten the dire human rights situation of Afghan women and has neglected the fact that their future role within the country will have a significant impact on attaining a truly sustainable and long-lasting peace. The politicisation of Afghan women has been a phenomenon that has repeated itself throughout the course of Afghanistan's history. By taking a closer look at the role that Afghan women have played within the country, I offer an Indian-feminist framework to deconstruct the current situation. I argue that only by taking an honest look into Afghanistan's history and both recognising and eliminating the culture of exclusion that has been imposed onto Afghan women can we set concrete foundations for the way forward.

Politicising Women: A Long and Diverse Practice

Gaining its independence from the British in 1919, Afghanistan joined the non-aligned movement in the post-war era. Agnostic to the East and the West, the country continued to receive aid from both spheres of influence.

Poverty has been prevalent throughout Afghanistan's history, with a long reign of feudalism carving Afghanistan into small fiefdoms and a centralised power base in Kabul. Afghanistan went through a series of key shifts in power that eventually led to the Soviet Invasion of 1979. Before the invasion, there were signs of progress for women. Afghanistan had a number of women in cabinet; in the country's urban cities women were going to school; and there was a female presence within the police force. In 1973, Mohammed Daoud Khan seized power from the long-time monarch, King Zahir Shah. Daud was launched into power with the help of the USSR-backed Parcham faction.[1] His main goal was to push for modernisation and to revisit the ethnic-based territorial dispute over Pashtunistan with Afghanistan's southern neighbour, Pakistan.

It was during this time that Afghanistan was reducing the role of Parcham in the government, undoubtedly disgruntling the USSR.[2] This rift in relations guided Daoud Khan to play down the Pashtunistan issue and improve relations with Pakistan, as well as open ties with Iran and Western nations. He wanted to reduce the Soviet role within Afghanistan and affirmed this when he banned all other political parties after establishing his own Mili-Ghorzang.[3] This was a critical blow to the USSR-supported People's Democratic Party of Afghanistan (PDPA), which was gaining momentum with the uniting of Parcham and Khalq parties in Afghanistan. After engaging in a tense discourse with USSR President Brezhnev, and declaring that, "[Afghanistan] will never allow [The Soviet Union] dictating to us how to run our country, and whom to employ in Afghanistan," Daoud made it clear that he wanted to reduce Afghan-Soviet relations. He underscored his political decision by ordering the arrest of PDPA leaders for reasons of subversion. This subsequently led to the coup d'état by the PDPA and the assassination of Daud and his family.

Termed "The Saur Revolution", the USSR-backed government, led by Nur Mohammed Taraki who was the leader of the Khalq faction of the PDPA, and Babrak Karmal, who led the Parcham division, sought radical change in Afghanistan. It was within this time frame where they began utilising women's rights as a political tool.

Rather than trying to bring about long-term, substantive programmes to empower women, the regime implemented superficial gestures such as promoting women entertainers. Prior to the PDPA regime, as a part of weddings, the groom was required to give the women a mehr (money or property), which would be in her name. The regime set a limit of 300 Afghanis for a women's mehr, the reduction of which further exacerbated women's financial insecurity. The PDPA also went so far as to place limits on the cost of weddings, often raiding receptions and sometimes looting the venues. This inherently stripped the Afghan people of their freedom of expression and association. The PDPA also tried to implement its programmes by force. For example, the regime required women to attend a literacy programme. When government officials met with resistance in Kuner Province, they slaughtered hundreds of people in one night.

Afghan Women at the Crossroads of Geopolitics

At the same time that the PDPA was mobilising, mujahideen factions were forming in resistance to the communist political expansion, with Islam as their choice of political ideology. In reaction to the actions of the PDPA, when they took over the area, the mujahideen opposed formal education. The era saw the spread of pan-Islamic ideas throughout the Middle East and the rise of a religious national leader in Iran and the Islamisation of President Zia in Pakistan. The USSR saw Afghanistan as a fellow Soviet state, although it was neither part of the eastern bloc nor a true socialist state. It was within the same time frame that the PDPA continued to highlight the party's façade of female empowerment. The PDPA underscored the high numbers of Afghan women enrolled in universities by ignoring the dwindling number of Afghan males enrolled, as many had left Kabul in exodus, escaping execution by the ruling communist regime.

On December 24, 1979 the first Russian planes arrived in Afghanistan. The Soviets proclaimed that they had decided to grant the PDPA's "insistent request ...[for] immediate aid and support the struggle against external aggression."[4] They also added that the Soviet contingent would be completely pulled out of Afghanistan when the demand was no longer needed. The invasion ignited the outrage of the non-communist world.

The US saw the invasion as a clear defiance against the West and gross disregard for détente. The timing of the Soviet invasion exacerbated the US outlook on Soviet intentions.

The Soviet invasion jolted American beliefs that the USSR was taking advantage of declining American presence in the region following the Islamic Revolution in Iran. It fuelled US concerns that Soviet control of Afghanistan would be a major step toward overland access to the Indian Ocean and to domination of the Asian subcontinent.[5] The invasion took place at a time when "the Americans were in the mood to be upset."[6] In what can be referred to as the "red template syndrome", the Soviet occupation of Afghanistan was seen as a threat to the security of the oil-rich Persian Gulf.[7] Four days after the invasion, the United States approved a broader plan instructing the CIA to provide military supplies and humanitarian aid to the Afghan freedom fighters (mujahideen).[8] On January 4, 1979, US President Carter addressed the nation on the strategic significance of the invasion, saying that a Soviet-occupied Afghanistan threatened not only the world's oil supplies but also the very security of the United States. Carter solidified US support for the Afghan mujahideen, and Carter and the Congress were united in their opposition to the Soviet Invasion.[9] The humanitarian aid that was being sent was tailored towards funding and training the mujahideen to fight in what would become a proxy war between the US and USSR.

The Carter Doctrine had as its premise that "any attempt by any outside force to gain control of the Persian Gulf region would be regarded as an assault on the vital interests of the United States, and would be repelled by any means necessary, including the use of military force."[10] Carter's strategy was designed to address Soviet advances in the "Third World", but was also recognition that America's security had become interdependent with the security of Western Europe, the Far East, and the Middle East.[11] It also gave birth to the Rapid Deployment Joint Task Force (RDF), which allayed the widespread fear that the US could not fulfil its commitment within the Gulf region.

Diplomatic measures were also taken by the US to further ostracise the Soviet Union. Carter, in a bid to attract European support, highlighted the human rights aspect concerning the invasion. The Carter Administration urged the UN to investigate Soviet human rights abuses in Afghanistan. The United States boycotted the 1980 Moscow Olympics, and imposed sanctions on the supply of services and equipment to the USSR in connection with the games.[12]

Pakistan was key to launching the CIA's covert aid to the mujahideen. Lethal equipment was first shipped from the US to Pakistan in January 1980.[13] By the end of the Carter Administration in January 1981, the United States was spending roughly $ 60 million per year in military aid to Afghanistan through Pakistani channels.[14] Pakistan took a primary role in helping the US because it was receiving both economic aid and fulfilling its political interests in Afghanistan.[15] President Ronald Reagan continued the covert war against the Soviet Union in Afghanistan, which accounted for 80 per cent of the CIA's annual covert operations expenditures.[16] The Reagan administration proposed $ 3.2 billion in aid to Pakistan to give it "confidence in [the U.S.] commitment to its security."[17] In return, the Pakistani intelligence service trained tens of thousands of mujahideen fighters in Pakistan from 1984 to 1987.

Other Middle Eastern nations played a role in aiding the US in training and supplying the mujahideen, including by providing fighters. Egypt trained Afghan guerrillas, and Iran was able to train and send monetary aid to the mujahideen.[18] Israel sold hundreds of tons of Soviet-made armaments, which it had captured in its 1982 incursion into Lebanon, to the United States for shipment to the mujahideen.[19] China had also sold many of its armaments to mujahideen fighters through Pakistan.[20] In this way, the mujahideen were supported by the United States and its allies. Saudi Arabia was also brought into the alliance against the USSR because of its willingness to augment American funds to the mujahideen. During the Carter Administration, Saudi Arabia matched the United States' $ 60 million per year expenditure in Afghanistan. For Saudi Arabia, this was a unique opportunity to gain influence in the region and to export its brand of ultra-conservative Islam termed Wahhabism.[21] Saudi Arabia over time became the United States' most important Middle Eastern backer, and Wahhabism was spread throughout the refugee camps they funded.

From Cold War to Extremism

Much like the PDPA, the mujahideen at this time were using Afghan women as a political tool. Only, instead of communism, their tool was politicised Islam. It was during this period of brutal guerilla warfare that human insecurity spread throughout the country. Drought and access to food exacerbated nationwide poverty levels, and many Afghan families were selling or forcing their daughters into marriages due to the lack of security or for financial gain. On occasion, women kidnapped by fighters were doubly victimised when they were precluded from returning home due to social stigma. Though widespread human insecurity was prevalent throughout Afghanistan, Afghan women suffered the brunt of the invasion. Their bodies became a weapon of war. The mujahideen fighters used the vulnerability of Afghan women to sell their vision of Afghanistan to the broader population, promising that they would ensure the safety of Afghans and their women.

The successive years of brutal conflict between communist and mujahideen factions led to a mass exodus of Afghan refugees pouring into neighbouring states and the western hemisphere. At this point, I myself was left a widow and single mother to my son after my husband was abducted. I continued my studies in Kabul and first practised medicine at the Wazir Akbar Khan Hospital, later relocating to Jaghori, a district of Ghazni province, free from the government. I opened my first clinic in 1982 with limited resources. The women of my village were adding to Afghanistan's high maternal mortality rates in high numbers, many dying of basic health complications that would take minutes to cure in an adequately equipped hospital. Médicins Sans Frontières (MSF) operated in Jaghori at the time, and, at my request, I received some basic medical supplies to sustain my practice and serve my community. I used every possible means of transportation, including donkeys, to reach and help people in need.

Pakistan witnessed an influx of nearly 6 million Afghan refugees who were given only limited emergency and humanitarian aid by the Pakistani government. With no formal education available in refugee areas, boys were sent to religious madrasas, which later gave rise of the Taliban. For female refugees the living conditions were particularly dire. There was little to no access to basic necessities such as washrooms, medical clinics, and education. The aid that was being distributed was both male and war-dominated. By end of 1984, I migrated to Pakistan as a refugee and was practising in a hospital based in Quetta as well going to the refugee camps twice a week. I distinctly remember treating a woman who was battling pre-eclampsia, a treatable maternal complication, and who later died. It was this very case that prompted me to open the first women's clinic in 1987 for Afghan female refugees living in Quetta, Pakistan. I later in 1989 opened the second hospital, Shuhada hospital, for women and children in another location of the town. Later on, I opened the first school for refugee girls there in 1990.

The continuous attempts of the Soviet Union trying to control Afghanistan was becoming a bleeding financial wound, pressing the USSR to find a way to withdraw from Afghanistan—very similar to the peace talks of today. For Gorbachev, in order to revive the Soviet economy, he needed to end the occupation of Afghanistan whether by victory or retreat.[22] After a series of Soviet-American talks, under terms of an agreement signed in Geneva on April 14, 1988, the Soviet Union withdrew its troops from Afghanistan.[23] The expulsion of the Soviets was celebrated as one of the most sensational US victories of the Cold War. It was a triumph at a huge cost. The invasion had led to over 14,000 Soviet casualities, and an estimated Russian war cost of $ 76-$ 152 billion.[24] For Afghanistan the death toll was 1 million, with over 6 million Afghans both internally and externally displaced.[25]

By 1992, when Dr. Najibullah's regime fell and the mujahideen took over central power in Kabul, the US abandoned Afghanistan. The status of Afghan women went from bad to worse. One of the new government's first decrees was making the hijab mandatory. Though the mujahideen allowed women to continue attending school, female news reporters were barred from being visually represented on television. The screen showed only the picture of a rose, as the women would read the daily news. Later on, female reporters were banned from reading the news altogether. In the series of international conferences that followed, the 1994 Cairo Conference on Population and Development and the 1995 Beijing

International Conference on Women, there was no Afghan government representation.

The Taliban began garnering state influence in 1994 and eventually took over centralised power in 1996. One of their first mandates was to close schools and public baths for Afghan women and girls, beginning in Afghanistan's southeast province of Kandahar. As they continued to take over swaths of the country, they systematically revoked the rights of women and girls. Education became outlawed and women were denied work outside of the house and access to adequate health care. This was in part due to the monetary aid flowing in from Arab states, such as Saudi Arabia, which called for the segregation of men and women and the active implementation of its extreme brand of Wahhabism.

Under Taliban rule, children were prohibited from making and playing with small toys, which were deemed unlawful live representations. Sports fields were no longer used for leisure, but as stages of public executions. Afghan women were ordered to wear the blue burqas ensuring no part of their body was visible. Many Afghan women who lived through this era can recount a time where she was whipped or beaten by the Taliban due to her shoes mistakenly showing or for merely making noise, which the Taliban deemed as distractions.

The extent of female oppression in Afghanistan, for the most part, fell on deaf Western ears, with little attention in Europe and North America. Emma Bonino, who was a European Commissioner at the time, was shocked at the status and condition of women in Afghanistan after her first visit to Kabul in 1997 when she and her companions were arrested as they were taking photos of a female hospital. She launched the campaign, "A Flower for the Women of Kabul", in 1998 and called upon "member governments of the United Nations, as well as all international organizations, to do all in their power to help restore the basic human rights of women in Afghanistan."[26] Alongside the US Feminist Majority Foundation, I joined Bonino in Brussels at a press conference for International Women's Day. I took part in the conference wearing a burqa for my own security, which in hindsight reminds me of the painful struggles I and many other Afghan women have gone through in fighting for our basic freedom and human rights.

In the United States, the Feminist Majority in 1997 launched a Campaign to Stop Gender Apartheid in Afghanistan, working in collaboration with human rights and Afghan women-led organisations and women members of Congress. The Feminist Majority Foundation's campaign generated media attention to the plight of women and girls under the Taliban and mobilised grassroots activity to galvanise Congressional action and press President Clinton not to recognise the Taliban regime.

From Extremism to Intervention

I will highlight here three key realities. First, that Afghanistan had now become a training camp for terrorists, mentioning that they will eventually launch attacks westward. Second, the drug trade was flourishing, particularly opium harvesting and exporting, thriving as a cash crop in Afghanistan and destabilising regional security. Third, and finally, Afghanistan had become the biggest prison in the world for women and girls.

After the tragic terrorist attacks which occurred on September 11, 2001 on US soil, American attention turned to Afghanistan once more. The reality of Afghan women's rights became a tool for the US government to garner national support for the intervention to remove the Taliban from power. Images of Afghan women allowed US officials to depict the brutality of the Taliban, which made Americans more sympathetic to Afghan women and enraged by the socio-political status of the country, once more politicising Afghan women, this time to establish an "us versus them" mentality, employing the US as the actor in charge of dealing with the situation.[27]

Early US presidential statements with respect to Afghanistan were heavily focused on the plight of Afghan women. President George W. Bush gave speeches, saying that "the people of Afghanistan have suffered under the most brutal regimes in modern history; a regime allied with terrorists and a regime at war with women,"[28] and that "[US] responsibilities to the people of Afghanistan have not ended. [The US] will work for a new era of human rights and human dignity in that country."[29]

Most notably, First Lady Laura Bush addressed the issue of women's rights in a weekly radio presidential address. Her powerful remark, "our hearts break for the women and children in Afghanistan, but also because in Afghanistan we see the world the terrorist would like to impose on the rest of us"[30] transformed the Taliban into a US national security threat. Following Ms. Bush's speech, Cherie Blair, the wife of British Prime Minister Tony Blair, along with other female cabinet ministers, made a similar plea on behalf of Afghan women claiming, "the women in Afghanistan are as entitled as the women in any country are to have the same hopes and aspirations for ourselves and for our daughters."[31]

The brutal treatment of Afghan women was also visually emphasised by television and press reports. Photos of Afghan women wearing the blue burqas were a constant visual reminder for the Western public of the Taliban's extremist ideologies. Most notably, TIME magazine's publication of the young Afghan woman whose ears and nose were cut off gave Western readers a chilling image of Taliban brutality.[32] The headline, "What happens if we leave Afghanistan" further legitimised the continuity of the war.[33]

The Afghan Women and Children Relief Act of 2001 supported reconstruction of Afghanistan, emphasising the human rights of Afghan women and girls.[34] The efforts of Representatives Carolyn Maloney (D-NY) and Sheila Jackson Lee (D-TX) and a coalition of US women's groups led by the Feminist Majority resulted in the allocation of $ 60 million for programmes for Afghan women and girls and $ 5 million for the Afghan Independent Human Rights Commission in 2003 as a part of an emergency supplemental appropriations package. Furthermore, the creation of the United Nations Assistance Mission in Afghanistan (UNAMA) registered an institution to uphold international norms throughout the rebuilding process of Afghanistan. More specifically, one of its key mandates is to "focus on combating violence against women and enable their participation in the public sphere."[35] Furthermore, after the removal of the Taliban from power, sweeping reforms were underway to catapult Afghanistan into a "new", modern society.[36]

The condition of Afghan women post-Taliban has improved. However, we continue to struggle for gender parity, equal access to opportunity and upward mobility. The isolation of most Afghan women remains entrenched in the "social structure, custom and culture of warlord anarchism."[37] Afghan women continue to suffer in uneven numbers from weak social, economic and health factors worsened by widespread insecurity and violence at the hands of hostile non-state actors such as the Taliban and ISIS.[38] Furthermore, the insurgent strategy has violently targeted Afghan women in positions of power and influence, mostly because we symbolise an epitomised "betrayal" to the older order of the Taliban.[39] This is because of our active and visible participation in what they deem to be "new" Afghanistan. The socio-political climate within Afghanistan remains unstable. It is therefore imperative for us Afghan women to channel our fears into tangible improvements that will endure regardless of what government comes into power in Afghanistan.

Peace and Feminism in Tomorrow's Afghanistan: Recommendations

Feminism within the Afghan context is centred on a notion of inclusivity. This means it must be an idea in which Afghan women and men can find themselves represented, irrespective of their sexual orientation, ethnicity, religion, or economic background. Given the culture of isolation that has historically framed Afghan women's participation, we must employ inclusion in our dealings especially with regard to peace.

The experiences and barriers faced by Afghan women must be taken into consideration when we try to systematically and institutionally further our advancement in society. Gender equality in the Afghan sense must mean that Afghan children are brought into the world without being socially trained to conform to gender roles that have been molded and politicised by successive years of conflict. The reality is that Afghanistan is at an intersection of immense structural change, with the continued presence of repressive identities threatening the processes of state building that would afford all citizens, women and men, the ability to realise their potential as humans. This being said, the ongoing peace negotiations must take into account and be mindful of five key elements.

To begin, the process must be based on an honest narration of history, and therefore it requires time and inclusive deliberations. This is to say that Afghanistan is in need of a long-lasting peace, not a "quick-fix". A short-term solution will result in continued conflict that threatens to poison not only Afghanistan, but also the region and the world.

Secondly, good governance must be central. The Afghan people must be afforded the ability to be represented by a functioning state that can account for their human needs. This includes basic necessities such as education and health services. An indication of a healthy democracy and social fabric is when the government has the capacity to provide basic social and civil services.

This leads to the third recommendation, which is ensuring that citizens have fair and equal access to justice, which includes a functioning rule of law within Afghanistan. Political inclusion of women. Currently, citizens have a low level of trust in the justice system with corruption being an exacerbating force. However, should Afghanistan be given the opportunity to pursue both truth in reconciliation and transitional justice, public confidence in the state structure would increase throughout the country. Rebuilding citizen trust and confidence is essential. Accountability, justice and mechanisms to heal the wounds of the victims must be central to the peace process. The peace process must incorporate the meaningful participation of Afghan women and Afghan victims of war and terrorism. Their role within the peacebuilding process must not just be symbolic, but substantive and commensurate with their stake in the outcome of negotiations.

Finally, and most importantly, human rights in Afghanistan must remain non-negotiable. It is imperative to highlight that peace and freedom go hand in hand and that one cannot manifest without the other. Afghanistan cannot be allowed to regress on the human rights progress that it has made over the past seventeen years. But we must recognise that upholding universal principles of human rights is a shared responsibility among Afghans, the international community and United Nations agencies, and must not be sacrificed or exchanged with the excuse of stability. As outlined in the preamble of the United Nations charter, regional and international actors involved in Afghanistan must be committed to "reaffirm faith in fundamental human rights, in the dignity and worth of the human person, in the equal rights of men and women and of nations large and small."

Conclusion

As an Indian feminist, I view Afghani woman, as having faced great injustice throughout their life. As a young girl, they have been taught to believe that men were superior to women and that they could not be afforded the same opportunities as the men. Our Afghani sisters have fought for human rights and against discrimination in a country that has been ravaged by war and shaped by the political forces of patriarchy and global hegemons. They have been threatened by militia forces and told to close down Afghani women's operations of educating Afghan girls.

We must not lose sight of the fact that the promotion and protection of human rights, particularly of women and girls, is key to sustainable peace and development. This can be achieved if we work together. If we have learned anything from history, it is that the sacrifice of human rights and women's rights in the name of political expediency will result in conflict and abuses and will fuel the culture of impunity.

Latest Developments: Perspective of Indian Feminist

On August 15, 2021, the Taliban entered Kabul and took the city, and Indians knew from this moment the life for women and girls in Afghanistan would change for worse. Over the past month, we have been seeing day by day how the lives of women and girls have been impacted. Fear has been inflicted upon women in Afghanistan.

What we're hearing and seeing from Afghan women and girls is sheer terror. Women remember the 1990s and what it was like to live under Taliban rule. They have made broad statements that women's rights will be respected within the framework of Islam, but their actions have not inspired much confidence.

Since the Taliban took over power, a cabinet has been chosen that has no women. No women were included in the ministry. The Ministry for Women's Affairs has been abolished.

Afghan women have been at the forefront of fighting for their rights for centuries. Afghan women had the right to vote in 1919, before the United States gave women the right to vote. The 2004 constitution has gender equality as its basic feature.

UN Women in Afghanistan is committed to staying and delivering for Afghan women and girls. Firstly, this means engaging in advocacy to ensure that women's rights are protected and promoted and that Afghan women are not just talked about, but that they are heard from directly. The eyes of the world are on Afghanistan now, but that won't last forever. After the cameras of the world stop rolling on Afghanistan, the Taliban is going to exploit women to a greater extent.

Another key part of UN Women's work is supporting women's civil society and the women's movement in Afghanistan. We know that women's organisations are engines for progress and accountability, but that women's rights organisations only receive less than one per cent of overseas development assistance. We need to counter this trend by investing in women's civil society organisations.

We know that Afghan women experience some of the highest rates of violence globally, and most of that violence happens in the home. Nine out of 10 Afghan women experience at least one form of intimate partner violence in their lifetime, and that was before COVID-19. The pandemic has increased rates of violence against women across the globe, including in Afghanistan.

Finally, UN Women is working with the humanitarian system in Afghanistan to ensure a gender-sensitive humanitarian response to Afghanistan's triple crises of conflict, COVID-19, and climate. That means ensuring the needs of the most impacted women and girls are met, that women can participate fully in the design and delivery of the humanitarian response, and that data-driven evidence and analysis are used to ensure the response is effective for women and girls. Working with women's civil society organisations and women leaders, UN Women will make data-driven analysis available to national and international actors working in the country by releasing monthly survey results that look at the impact of the Taliban's rule on women and girls, effects on social and gender norms, and impacts for women's ability to access humanitarian services.

Afghanistan is confronting a crisis of the kinds of proportions that it may not have ever faced before. Half of the population is in need of some form of humanitarian assistance . One-third don't know where their next meal will come from. There is a risk of a fourth COVID-19 wave because of the collapsing health infrastructure.

The only way for Afghanistan to navigate these challenges is to ensure that all of its people are on board, men and women, coming together to find a way through crisis and catastrophe. Women's full participation and leadership in public and political life is critical for Afghanistan's future and long-term development, for sustaining peace, and for creating a vibrant economy that can bounce back from any crisis.

Indian feminists need to support their Afghani sisters even though through their writings and lobbying with Indian government and NRI women in Western countries to rescue Afghani sisters. They should be given refuge in India and other secular countries till the time a stable, secular government has been formed. Taliban has to be strongly opposed by Indian feminists. Women's rights are human rights and participation in it needs the support of the whole world.

Notes

1. Henry S. Bradsher, *Afghan Communism and Soviet Intervention* (Oxford: Oxford University Press, 1999), 18.
2. Ibid., 18.
3. Ibid., 19.
4. Nancy Peabody Newell and Richard S. Newell, *The Struggle for Afghanistan* (Ithaca, New York: Cornell University Press, 1981), 100.
5. Stanley Hoffman, *Dead Ends: American Foreign Policy in the New Cold War* (Cambridge, Massachusetts: Ballinger Publishers, 1983), 69.
6. Gabriella Grasseli, *British and American Responses to the Soviet Invasion of Afghanistan* (Vermont: Dartmouth Publishing Company, 1996), 120.
7. Ibid., 120.
8. Dennis Kux, *The United States and Pakistan 1979-2000* (Washington: Woodrow Wilson Center Press, 2001), 252.
9. Andrew Hartman, "'The Red Template': US Policy in Soviet-Occupied Afghanistan," *Third World Quarterly* 23, no. 3 (2002), 467-89, 471.
10. Grasseli, n. 6, 121.
11. Ibid., 163.
12. Ibid., 25.
13. Bradsher, n. 1, 215.
14. Ibid., 216.
15. Ibid., 214.

16. Ibid., 218.
17. Hartman, n. 9, 478.
18. Bradsher, n. 1, 216.
19. Ibid., 216.
20. Kurt Lohbeck, *Holy War, Unholy Victory: Eyewitness to the CIA's Secret War in Afghanistan* (Washington: Regnery Publishing, 1993), 54.
21. Hartman, n. 9, 478.
22. Anthony Arnold, *The Fateful Pebble: Afghanistan's Role in the Fall of the Soviet Empire* (California: Presidio Press, 1987), 187.
23. Bradsher, n. 1, 263.
24. Hartman, n. 9, 467.
25. European Community Humanitarian Office Press Release, "'A Flower for the Women of Kabul'—An International Campaign for the Women of Afghanistan" (Brussels, 1998).
26. Ole Weaver, "Securitization and Desecuritization", in Ronnie D. Lipshutz (ed.), *On Security* (New York: Columbia University Press, 1995), 46-86.
27. George W. Bush, "Remarks at the Signing Ceremony for Afghan Women and Children Relief Act of 2001" (Speech at The National Women's Museum in the Arts, Washington, DC, on December 12, 2001).
28. Ibid.
29. Ibid.
30. Alex J. Bellamy et al. (eds.), *Security and the War on Terror* (New York, NY: Routledge, 2008), 48.
31. Axel Heck and Gabi Schlag, "Securitizing Images: The Female Body and the War in Afghanistan", *European Journal of International Relations* 19, no. 4 (April 2012): 891-914.
32. Ibid.
33. Office of International Women's Issues, US Department of State, "U.S. Support for Afghan Women, Children, and Refugees" (Report Submitted to Congress), Washington, June 22, 2004, at https://2001- 2009.state.gov/g/wi/rls/33787.htm
34. "Violence Against Women", last modified October 23, 2013, United Nations Assistance Mission in Afghanistan Website, "Human Rights" (Web Page), last viewed 2019, at https://unama.unmissions.org/ human-rights
35. Maliha Chishti, "Gender and the Development Battlefield in Afghanistan: National Builders versus Nation Betrayers", *Comparative Studies South Asia, Africa and the Middle East* 30, no. 2 (2010), 4.
36. Marion Iris Young, "The Logic of Masculinist Protection: Reflection on the Current Security State", *Journal of Women in Culture & Society* 29, no. 1 (Autumn 2003): 1-25.
37. Chishti, n. 36, 1.
38. Ibid., 11.
39. Ibid., 11.

4. India's Stakes, Challenges and Strategy in the Aftermath of Talibans in Afghanistan

Neeraj Singh Manhas

India's goals in Afghanistan are calibrated to balance domestic, regional, and global interests. Countering Pakistan's influence is one of India's objectives, but it has a wide variety of interests in Afghanistan. The main objective of Delhi in Afghanistan is to prevent Pakistani-backed extremists from launching attacks on Indian soil or against Indian interests (for example, against its diplomatic missions in Afghanistan). Security within Afghanistan and concerted measures to halt terrorists operating with impunity beyond Afghanistan's borders must be our combined efforts in Afghanistan, remarked India's Permanent Representative to the UN in July 2008. Four months later, in November 2008, strikes by Pakistan-backed Lashkar-e-Taiba (LeT) members in Mumbai reinforced India's resolve to prevent similar attacks, even by military means.

Pakistan will be free to utilise Afghanistan as a safe haven and training ground for anti-Indian radicals once US soldiers leave. As the Indian publication *Mint* editorialised,

Once certain of a sympathetic administration in Kabul, Islamabad will unleash all terrorists on India. Terrorist groups will be emboldened to strike our cities more frequently as a result of this.

Delhi wants a stable, democratic, multi-ethnic Afghan government that can control the whole country, keep peace, stop the Taliban from coming back, and lessen anti-India extremism in the country, so this can't happen. India, on the other hand, needs to fight back against Pakistani political power in order to make this happen. When Arun Sahgal, who was a retired Indian Brigadier and once led the Indian military's long-term strategic planning staff, wrote this, he said it "from the Indian point of view".

Preventing Pakistan from becoming the exclusive arbitrator of Afghan political and strategic discourse is critical, as it would strengthen the proxy war against India and promote Islamic radicalism in Afghanistan.

Significantly Expand Access to Central Asia

Each country needs new energy sources to keep their economies growing and getting better. India has grown at a rate of more than 7% a year since 1997, making it the world's second-fastest-growing energy market. By 2030, the country will need to import more than 80% of its fuel. The proposed Turkmenistan-Afghanistan-Pakistan-India (TAPI) pipeline would run 1,000 miles and cost $ 7.6 billion. It would carry 33 billion cubic metres of Turkmen gas a year, which would bring Afghanistan $ 1.4 billion a year in transit fees. India and Pakistan would each get 14 bcm/y, which would be 1.5 per cent of India's total annual energy consumption and 15 per cent of Pakistan's total annual energy consumption each year. Both India and Pakistan want to keep Afghanistan stable so that they can get energy from Central Asia. The TAPI pipeline must cross Afghanistan, so both countries have a lot of reasons to keep Afghanistan safe.

Demonstrate Global Interests and Project Power

India's growth and integration into the global economy have made commercial and trade goals more important to Delhi in its foreign policy. People in India think their country is a powerful country that should try to change the world around them. Shahrbanou Tadjbakhsh, a researcher at the Peace Research Institute Oslo, says that India's desire to be an extra-regional power is "legitimate". This is "commensurate with the growth of its economy".

Delhi has used its military for a long time to show its power all over the world. More than 100,000 Indian troops have been part of 40 UN peacekeeping missions since the 1950s, and more than 8,000 of them are still there today. The Indian Navy has sent ships to fight piracy off the coast of Somalia, even though these ships aren't part of the multinational naval task force. Even in the areas of South and Central Asia, India's military has become more and more active. It built an air force base in Tajikistan. From there, it sends humanitarian aid, construction materials, and other goods into Afghanistan. The base also allows it to show military strength in Central Asia. During the political turmoil in Nepal in 2011, India trained Kyrgyz troops in peacekeeping skills and set up an agreement to fight terrorism together. In early 2012, India relaunched military cooperation with Nepal that had been halted because of the country's political turmoil. India has also sent a small number of security forces to Afghanistan, mostly to protect Indian diplomatic missions and aid projects.

As a world power, India must have a bigger say in South Asia if it wants to be taken seriously and many Indians agree with the viewpoint. "Afghanistan is a test for India's rise as a regional and global power," says Harsh V. Pant in a new book. "India's ability to deal with problems in its own backyard will in the end keep it from becoming a major global power." An ex-Indian Army deputy chief of staff says, "If India wants to be a major player in the region, it can't just leave Afghanistan. It has to stay."

India's Strategies in Afghanistan

India has a variety of ways to further its interests in Afghanistan. Aside from pursuing political and economic influence in Kabul, Delhi seeks to win Afghan hearts and minds by offering massive development assistance and projecting its considerable "soft power".

Attempt to Establish Political Influence in Afghanistan

India has attempted several measures to influence Afghan politics.

- **Back the Karzai Regime.** To prevent Pakistani-backed terrorists from returning to Afghanistan, India actively seeks influence in the Afghan government. It has helped strengthen the Karzai administration, create multi-ethnic democratic institutions, and increase the Afghan security forces' capabilities.

- **Establish a Diplomat.** India has a strong diplomatic presence in Afghanistan to represent its interests. After the Taliban fell, Delhi reopened its embassy in Kabul and consulates in Kandahar and Jalalabad, and later consulates in Herat and Mazar-e-Sharif, the western and northern commercial hubs of Afghanistan. Indian diplomats can now meet local authorities, boost trade and investment, and learn about regional developments. The Foreign Ministry, Islamabad claims that "Indian consulates in Jalalabad and Kandahar constitute a veritable base for RAW [Research and Analysis Wing, India's intelligence arm] and its accessories." India denies the claim, whether it is accurate or not.
- **Keep the Northern Card in the Rear Pocket.** During the Taliban's tenure, India backed the NA (Northern Alliance), which was dominated by Tajiks and Uzbeks and opposed Pakistani-backed mujahideen. The Indian military built a field hospital in Tajikistan for its forces to utilise. Some in India advised the government to restart backing for former friends to confront Pashtun insurgents and prevent a Taliban resurgence. Rather than prevent Pashtun hostility, such a measure may inspire it. This is because, getting involved in the hostility would further encourage insurgents to attack Indian soil. Resuming military backing for the NA might aggravate tensions between Tajik-majority northern Afghanistan and Pashtun-majority Kabul, resulting in a "hotter" proxy war. However, if Pakistan boosts its backing for anti-Indian terrorists, India may choose to retaliate in kind; if Pakistan encourages its proxies to become more active in India, India may do the same in Afghanistan.
- **Aid Afghan Political Reconciliation.** A reconciliation with the Taliban might allow Pakistani-backed militants to resume using Afghanistan as a safe haven for planning and launching strikes against India and its interests. "India's security interest revolves around denying any political or military space to the ISI-backed Taliban and other such hardline groups," a leading Indian research tank wrote. Having failed to stop the Taliban from operating in Kabul, India has softened its stance to retain some influence. Due to the fact that multinational peace talks kept the door open for a Taliban involvement in government, India decided to accept the idea of speaking with insurgent leaders who

abandoned violence. With or without a government, such a significant shift in posture "represent[ed] an acknowledgment in New Delhi that it will need to have links with power brokers in Afghanistan." Contrary to popular belief, India's authorities determined that they would be better positioned to fight Pakistani influence if they participated in the reconciliation effort rather than opposed it from the outside.

Contribute to Development and Pursue Economic Influence

To further marginalise the Taliban and boost security, the Karzai government must develop Afghanistan's economy and job market. In a November 2011 Asia Foundation poll, 45 per cent of Afghan respondents said unemployment, poverty, or a bad economy were the country's worst problems. With the belief that "social and economic development is important to ensuring Afghanistan becomes a source of regional peace," the Indian government has utilised a variety of economic policy strategies to foster stability and strengthen Indian influence in Afghanistan:

- **Foreign aid.** India offers the most foreign aid to Afghanistan. It is Afghanistan's sixth greatest donor and its largest South Asian donor. Delhi had pledged $ 1.3 billion in aid to Afghanistan as of early 2011, with other pledges bringing the total to $ 2 billion since 2001. Infrastructure, education, training, health care, agriculture, telecommunications, electricity generation, and civil aviation are among President Karzai's development goals. Small-scale community projects to large-scale power generation and transmission facilities. Despite India's desire to keep assisting Kabul in growth, the country's lack of security has hampered new project development. In fact, India had announced no substantial projects for two to three years prior to June 2011. Delhi sent 500 Indo-Tibetan Border Police (ITBP) members to secure Indian development workers and diplomatic facilities after a string of high-profile attacks, but the unrest in Afghanistan may necessitate further forces.
- **Trade.** This was a huge deal because one-quarter of Afghanistan's exports go to India, and bilateral trade is set to hit $ 1 billion by 2012. Due to Pakistan's border restrictions, Delhi must currently transfer products to Afghanistan via Iran. If Islamabad lifts this ban, Indian-Afghan trade will skyrocket.

- **Private investment.** Notably, 14 Indian corporations bid on a $ 6 billion iron mining contract in Bamyan province in late 2011. President Karzai encouraged Indian Prime Minister Manmohan Singh to encourage more Indian investment at the SAARC summit in the Maldives in November 2011, while Afghan Commerce and Industries Minister Anwar-Ul-Haq Ahady did the same in Delhi the month before. This bodes well for further bilateral investment expansion in the coming years.

This strategy is clearly intended to undercut Pakistani power in Afghanistan while highlighting Indian generosity, expanding trade, and gaining political advantage. In 2008-2009, the Indian Border Roads Organization (BRO) built a 220-km road between Zaranj and Delaram, connecting the main Herat-Kandahar highway with existing routes heading to the Iranian port of Chabahar. The route will also be far faster than the current network that connects Afghanistan to the Pakistani ports of Karachi and Gwadar. To help Indian corporations access Afghanistan's projected $ 1 trillion in minerals and raw resources, Delhi plans to create a train link from Hajigak, in Bamyan province, to Chabahar through Zaranj. India is also collaborating with Iran to create a 600-km road from Chabahar to Zahedan, near the southwestern border of Afghanistan. Although these lines will speed up the delivery of Afghan goods to major ports, the main gain will go to India. As a result of the new channel, Islamabad will be unable to ban Indian exports to Afghanistan and diminish the relevance of Pakistan's Gwadar port, which was built at a high cost with significant Chinese funding. The considerable security problems involved with these road and rail infrastructure projects emphasise India's strategic interest in securing access to Afghan minerals and markets. These roads travel through Taliban-controlled Nimroz region, allowing the Taliban (and likely their Pakistani sponsors) to impede Indian trade. To make these transit linkages genuinely effective, either the region's security be strengthened (possibly by Indian security troops protecting Indian development projects) or the Taliban be enticed to allow business to pass unmolested.

Regionalise Afghan Security and Stability Solutions

So that all nations in the region might "advance together through free trade, open borders, and regional economic integration", India pursued regional solutions to Afghanistan's security and stability concerns. According to one Indian think tank researcher, this multilateral approach "allows Kabul to be more independent and less subject to Pakistani arm twisting" while also reducing Islamabad's influence over Afghan issues.

Delhi's regional strategy has included promoting Afghanistan's inclusion in SAARC, both to institutionalise its integration with its neighbours and to promote greater bilateral trade. Regional economic activity of up to $ 2 billion, including $ 600 million for Afghanistan, could result from Afghan economic integration. Afghanistan becomes a feasible land link between India and the energy-rich CARs.

They did, however, agree on one important regional project that would benefit both India and Pakistan: the 1,000-mile TAPI gas pipeline. Having a stable Afghanistan is important for both countries, as their energy needs expand.

Project Power

India is debating whether to deploy more security forces to protect its aid and investment initiatives in Afghanistan. This question is part of a larger debate over how India can project power in South Asia and beyond. "The challenge confronting Indian policy-makers on Afghanistan is not restricted to the country's special interests and engagement in reconstruction activities," notes Indian researcher Shantie Mariet D'Souza.

For example, safeguarding sea lines of communication utilised for marine trade and energy supplies has become an increasingly important part of Indian military strategy. Aircraft carriers and long-range bombers capable of mid-air refuelling have been acquired, and military leaders have shown interest in expanding access to ports throughout the Indian Ocean. Indian military capabilities remain limited, and recent overseas deployments have been largely humanitarian, such as the 2006 evacuation of South Asian residents from Lebanon and the 2004 delivery of aid to tsunami-hit Indonesia, Sri Lanka and the Maldives.

India aspires to impact regional developments and project power by playing a major role in Afghanistan's security and economic growth. Indian Foreign Secretary Nirupama Rao stated that India's rise as a global power necessitates "a peaceful and stable external environment", implying that India views Afghan stability as critical to accomplishing its strategic aims. According to Harsh V. Pant of King's College London, "the success of India's Afghanistan strategy will determine if India can emerge as a provider of regional security in South Asia." Delhi can also influence developments in the CARs through Afghanistan, both as a consumer of Central Asian oil and gas as a counterweight to Chinese and Russian power. India's operations in Afghanistan "regarding India's emerging potential to influence its wider strategic neighbourhood" earn Delhi recognition on the international stage by allowing it "to be, and to be viewed, as an extra-regional force advancing toward great power status," writes C. Christine Fair.

India also has a lot of soft power. The country's image is one of a multicultural, democratic nation with a strong economy and lively media. Its Bollywood film industry depicts opulent lifestyles and expensive festivities. In fact, an Indian soap opera dubbed into Dari was formerly one of Afghanistan's most popular television shows.

Grassroots Indian humanitarian efforts have also helped Afghans see India positively. Many of its aid efforts are purposely high-profile, such as the construction of a new parliament building and the donation of planes to Ariana Afghan Airlines. Aside from education and training initiatives, Delhi has provided free medical care to over 350,000 Afghans in less than two years. These and other reconstruction efforts have given India a ready-made channel to win Afghan hearts and minds. Partly to do this, Delhi has dispersed its development funding across Afghanistan, benefiting all regional and ethnic groups.

The Afghan elites with long-standing ties to India or to groups backed by it have also been targeted by Delhi. Former foreign minister and presidential candidate Abdullah Abdullah, former parliament speaker Younus Qanooni, and other prominent officials played key positions in the Indian-backed NA while the Taliban were in power.

Provide Military Assistance

The only way India has not imposed its will on Afghanistan is militarily. Although Delhi sent 500 ITBP troops to safeguard Indian humanitarian workers and diplomats, they were not on aggressive counter-insurgency or stability missions. Delhi has also reduced military involvement in Afghanistan for a variety of reasons. Most importantly, Indian policymakers recognise that sending soldiers to Afghanistan could strengthen anti-India extremists in Kashmir, which has become increasingly quiet in recent years.

After 2015, India appears to have become more proactive in its military collaboration with Afghanistan. In October 2011, Afghan President Hamid Karzai and Indian Prime Minister Manmohan Singh agreed to send light weaponry and COIN and high-altitude combat training to the Afghan army, police, and air force. The agreement does not call for Indian troops to be sent to Afghanistan and rather, despite Pakistan's reluctance, Delhi has opted to form a bilateral security relationship with Kabul by providing military training.

India's Strategies Are Effective

As a result of its success in furthering its strategic goals in Afghanistan, Delhi has sought to project political, economic, commercial, and cultural influence. Despite Pakistan's apparent displeasure, the Karzai government has strengthened political, economic, and diplomatic ties with Delhi. With India's help, Afghanistan will be able to access vital economic routes and energy markets in Central Asia, as well as join SAARC.

Delhi has garnered the respect of common Afghans as well as the Karzai government. Indian public support for its "no strings attached" reconstruction assistance, soft power projection, and outreach to all main Afghan ethnic groups is strikingly different from opinions of Pakistan. A 2009 ABC News/BBC poll indicated that "74% of Afghans favoured India, while 8% favoured Pakistan". By not participating in military efforts in Afghanistan, Delhi has cultivated an image as a positive contributor rather than an outside meddler. In contrast, 86 per cent of Afghans say Pakistan is a detrimental influence in Afghanistan.

However, a strong return of the Taliban might jeopardise most of Delhi's current and future measures. This would re-establish Kabul in Pakistan's orbit and effectively eliminate Indian aid, investment, and commerce in Afghanistan. That acceptance may have given India some leverage to prevent the inclusion of pro-Pakistan politicians in a future Kabul government, which, if successful, may temper these developments.

Implications for India

Indians increasingly believe that strengthening India's involvement in Afghanistan will help India strategically. However, while India's national security strategy calls for increased military power projection in the region, it is unclear if Delhi wants to increase its involvement in Afghanistan or take over tasks currently held by the US. This would cost a lot of money and men, and it would incite Islamabad to retaliate against India, which would virtually likely see it as a strategic defeat.

"As India continues to rise, Pakistan's reliance on Islamic militancy, the only tool it has to modify India's trajectory," C. Christine Fair told a congressional subcommittee in November 2011. If so, the threat of Pakistani-backed strikes should not discourage India from expanding its participation in Afghanistan to serve its larger strategic objectives.

Delhi's main question, then, is whether it thinks that the benefits of having more troops in Afghanistan outweigh the risks. India has already had a lot of debate about how to deal with Afghanistan in the future if the United States ever stops sending troops there. Some people say that India should cut its losses and stop promoting its own interests in Afghanistan before the security situation gets worse. But the general feeling in India is that the government has been too passive in promoting its own interests in Afghanistan. As a sign of this timidity, the government backed down when its opposition to talks with the Taliban was ignored at the London Conference in January 2010. Delhi didn't fight back after the conference. Instead, it said that it would talk to members of the Taliban who give up violence, stop terrorism, and follow the Afghan constitution. Columnists and commentators said the government was "defeatist" and couldn't or wouldn't use India's help with Afghanistan to help its own strategic goals.

Many Indians recognise that their country's great power ambitions are jeopardised if Delhi fails to preserve its essential interests at home. Many argue that if India wants to be a regional, much alone global, force, it must show it has the ability and political will to project its influence and influence events in Afghanistan. While most believe that a minimum level of political and economic participation is required, the subject of increased Indian military involvement in Afghanistan has sparked significantly more debate.

Continued political involvement, private investment, and development projects in Afghanistan are the least assertive options. In addition to contributing to Afghan security and economic growth, such activities boost Indian economic and commercial interests.

Amid a deteriorating security environment, Delhi may consider backup measures. India may quietly re-engage the NA by extending political, economic, and possibly military support. This would allow India to play its "northern card" by hampering the Taliban's influence-expanding operations. To support this strategy, supporters argue that India should coordinate with Russia, Iran, Uzbekistan, and Tajikistan, all of which oppose a resurgent Taliban, and open channels of communication with Taliban elements most likely to oppose Pakistani demands to train anti-India extremists in Afghanistan.

Additional security forces would be sent to protect India's diplomatic and commercial presence in Afghanistan. After the first Kabul explosion, the *Indian Express* editorialised in support of such a strategy, writing,

> After the Kabul tragedy, India must confront an essential issue it has evaded. New Delhi cannot keep increasing its economic and diplomatic operations in Afghanistan without increasing its military presence there. The Indian government must act promptly if withdrawal is not an option.

In this scenario, security missions would be strictly defensive, protecting Indian government employees, facilities, and investments. The objective might include protecting Indian individuals and facilities associated with private and public sector projects, but otherwise it would be a simple enlargement of the existing Indian deployment.

A third, bolder policy, would be for Delhi to keep training Afghan security forces in India. In addition to constructing a professional Afghan army, India would help improve Afghan counterterrorism capabilities to eradicate anti-India extremist safe havens.

The Indo-Afghan Strategic Partnership Agreement of October 2011 committed Delhi to educate modest numbers of Afghan security forces in counterterrorism and COIN methods. However, all training would take place in India, avoiding the controversial step of sending Indian troops to Afghanistan.

A fourth method would be to provide more training to Afghan military and police than agreed in the strategic partnership agreement. However, it warned that "such discussions should include consideration of possible counterproductive Pakistani reaction before embarking on any course of action."

A fifth option for Delhi would be to conduct security training within Afghanistan. While this would allow small teams of Indian instructors to train more Afghans, the presence of even a few Indian personnel on Afghan soil would raise Indo-Pak tensions.

The sixth and most aggressive plan would be to deploy Indian military to Afghanistan to train Afghan counterparts and conduct counter-Taliban operations. Delhi's use of "hard power" would take the fight to the militants, so to speak. Editor of the Indian journal *Pragati*, Sushant K. Singh, says:

> Afghanistan will become the new battlefield, away from Kashmir and India's mainland. India's anti-terrorist operations, particularly in Kashmir, will benefit greatly by targeting the jihadi base.

India would also be able to keep the northern trade routes to the CARs safe if it had a presence like this in the country. If India doesn't want to wait until 2014, it could start this strategy while US and NATO troops are already in Afghanistan.

But an Indian combat deployment to Afghanistan seems doubtful. By intervening to promote the interests of its historical Tajik and Uzbek partners at the expense of ethnic Pashtuns, an Indian military deployment would damage India's enormous goodwill in Afghanistan. Deploying a military intervention in Sri Lanka from 1987 to 1990, which cost 1,500 Indian lives and contributed to the Tamil Tigers assassinating Indian Prime Minister Rajiv Gandhi in 1991, would likely dissuade Indian decision makers from engaging in another low-intensity conflict that poses only indirect threats to Indian security. In October 2011, Indian External Affairs Minister S. M. Krishna remarked on Indian television that "India does not believe in sending soldiers to any country unless under UN auspices for peacekeeping purposes."

Also, as General McChrystal said, Islamabad would view any Indian military presence in Afghanistan as very provocative. An Indian presence will erode Pakistani military confidence in using Afghan territory for strategic depth. Even India's soft power initiatives caused alarm among Pakistan's military elites, as academic Harsh Pant argues. Senior Pakistani officials have previously condemned Delhi's offer to train Afghan security forces in Afghanistan or overseas. "Strategically, we cannot have an Afghan army on our western border with an Indian mindset and capabilities," said Pakistani Army Chief of Staff General Ashfaq Parvez Kayani. In light of this attitude, it becomes evident that substantial military training and operations by Indian troops inside Afghanistan would be too much for the Pakistani military.

However, Pakistan's retaliatory options are limited and may even harm its own interests. Islamabad might stifle Afghan exports to India, but this would hurt Kabul more than Delhi, thereby fuelling anti-Pakistani sentiment in Afghanistan. It might back out of the TAPI pipeline arrangement, but Pakistan needs Central Asian energy resources as much as India. Instead of TAPI, Pakistan might build a multi-billion-dollar pipeline to buy gas from neighbouring Iran, but growing international sanctions on Iran make this impossible. In addition to investing in the Gwadar port and supplying Chinese military equipment to the Pakistani army, Islamabad could seek more help from China.

To retaliate against Delhi, Islamabad may escalate insurgency activities in Kashmir or encourage further terrorist attacks à la 9/11. Given the history of Pakistani-backed extremist attacks on India, it seems unlikely that the Indian public would immediately link a future act of political violence with Delhi's expeditionary efforts in Afghanistan. To be fair, Americans (with a few vocal exceptions) have refused to accept Al-Qaeda's claim that the US government incited the 9/11 attacks through its policy toward the Muslim world.

However, India is unlikely to risk compromising the strategic benefits of a more proactive regional policy by sending combat troops or trainers to Afghanistan. Delhi is therefore more likely to use somewhat assertive actions while also creating backup plans to protect its bilateral relationship with Kabul. Indian diplomats and aid workers may be protected by additional paramilitary forces (such as the ITBP), but Delhi is unlikely to conduct large-scale training missions or conduct coordinated counterterrorism or COIN operations directly on Afghan soil.

India may also keep its political options open. For example, while continuing to back the Karzai administration, India will quietly try to cultivate relationships with Taliban individuals involved in the reconciliation process to avoid future enmity. Delhi may even decide to restart backing for its former NA partners in case a new Kabul regime, particularly one dominated by Pakistani-controlled Taliban, proves unfriendly. Moreover, despite highlighting the broad alignment of US and Indian views on Afghanistan, India is anticipated to work with Russia, Iran, Tajikistan, and Uzbekistan to prevent a future Taliban resurgence. If it hasn't already, Delhi may start building an infrastructure to support Baloch separatists operating in Pakistan as a non-attribution response to ISI-sponsored Islamist strikes on Indian interests and territory.

Conclusion

Currently, India and Pakistan have very distinct perspectives of Afghanistan and strive to advance very divergent interests through their various engagement policies. Islamabad sees Afghanistan as a battlefield for its conflict with India. To this purpose, Pakistan envisions a prominent role for the Taliban in a weak Kabul government, limiting Delhi's influence and preserving its use of Afghan territory as a training ground for militant proxy groups in its ongoing fight with India. Secondary goals include isolating

Afghanistan by preventing it from integrating into the South and Central Asian regional economy, and strengthening ties with Russia and Iran.

In contrast, India seeks peace and economic progress in Afghanistan to defend itself from terrorism, expand trade, secure Central Asian energy resources, and establish itself as a regional force. Pakistan wants an Afghan state that will undermine regional security; India wants an Afghan state that will promote political stability, security, economic growth, reconstruction and regional integration.

Afghanistan will certainly welcome enhanced Indian involvement in reconstruction and security in the short run. It is likely that President Karzai will accept Indian help and then take moves to accommodate Pakistan that at least partially nullify what India has achieved. Furthermore, a Taliban-dominated or Islamabad-influenced Kabul government would very probably want to sever ties with Delhi. This means that any Indian effort to deepen its role in Afghanistan must include a willingness to maintain obligations post-Karzai (and post-NATO).

India's aid to Afghan security forces, along with an increasingly assertive Indian participation in Afghanistan's economic and commercial development, gives the best prospect for entrenching—and even advancing—US gains in that region. Delhi can help improve security sector capacity, enhance political stability, increase trade, and most importantly, combat terrorist groups that directly threaten both India and the US. India would gain physical and economic security by assisting Afghanistan's reconstruction while sustaining and enhancing Washington's own efforts. To avoid a potential security vacuum, the US should encourage India to pursue a more assertive political, economic, and security strategy that includes greater military training and potentially deployment of Indian troops.

References

Abshire, David M., and Ryan Browne, "The Missing Endgame for Afghanistan: A Sustainable Post-bin Laden Strategy", *Washington Quarterly*, vol. 34, no. 4, Fall 2011, pp. 59-72. As of June 18, 2012, at http://csis.org/publication/twq-missing-endgame-afghanistan-sustainable-post-bin-laden-strategy

"Afghanistan Wants Indian Investments: Singh", *Daily Outlook Afghanistan*, November 14, 2011. As of June 15, 2012, at http://www.outlookafghanistan.net/news?post_id=2511

"Afghans Mourn After Killing of Peace Negotiator", Associated Press, May 14, 2012.

"After Kabul", *Indian Express*, July 8, 2008. As of June 19, 2012, at http://www.indianexpress.com/news/after-kabul/332675/0

Agreement Between the Governments of the Islamic Republic of Afghanistan and the Islamic Republic of Pakistan: Afghanistan-Pakistan Transit Trade Agreement, 2010 (APTTA), October 28, 2010. As of June 18, 2012, at http://www.commerce.gov.pk/APTTA/APTTA.pdf

Ahmad, Sardar, "28 Killed in Suicide Attack at India's Afghanistan Embassy", *Agence France-Presse*, July 7, 2008.

Alexander, Chris, "Afghanistan and Pakistan: A Strategy for Peace", *Options Politiques*, November 2010, pp. 30-35. As of June 18, 2012, at http://www.irpp.org/po/archive/nov10/alexander.pdf

Allbritton, Chris, "Holbrooke Hails Pakistan-U.S. Collaboration on Taliban", Reuters, February 18, 2010. As of June 18, 2012, at http://www.reuters.com/article/2010/02/18/us-pakistan-taliban-idUSTR E61H2QO20100218

Anand, Vinod, "Pakistan as a Factor in Afghan Stability", in R. K. Sawhney, Arun Sahgal, and Gurmeet Kanwal (eds.), *Afghanistan: A Role for India* (New Delhi: Centre for Land Warfare Studies, 2011), pp. 141-62.

Aneja, Atul, "India and Afghanistan: The Way Forward", *The Hindu*, January 4, 2011. As of June 15, 2012, at http://www.hindu.com/2011/01/04/stories/2011010451521200.htm

Anwar, Haris, "Pakistan Seeks Russia's Help to Finance Iran Gas Pipeline", Bloomberg, March 29, 2012. As of June 19, 2012, at http://www.bloomberg.com/n e w s/2012-03-29/pakistan-sending-team-to-russia-to-seek-iran-gas-pipeline-help.html

Arnoldy, Ben, "How the Afghanistan War Became Tangled in India vs. Pakistan Rivalry", *Christian Science Monitor*, January 20, 2011. As of June 28, 2012, at http://www.csmonitor.com/World/Asia-South-Central/2 011/0120/How-the-Afghanistan-war-became-tangled-in-India-vs.-Pakistan-rivalry

"Asim Hussain Paints a Dire Picture of the Gas Crisis", *Express Tribune*, January 3, 2012.

Baabar, Mariana, "Pakistan to Train Afghan Troops", *International News*, November 4, 2011. As of June 18, 2012, at http://www.thenews.com.pk/TodaysPrintDetail.aspx?ID=10067&Cat=13

Bajoria, Jayshree, "India-Afghanistan Relations", Council on Foreign Relations backgrounder, July 22, 2009. As of June 15, 2012, at http://www.cfr.org/india/india-afghanistan-relations/p17474

Barfield, Thomas J., *Afghanistan: A Cultural and Political History* (Princeton, NJ: Princeton University Press, 2010).

Bentley, John, "Leon Panetta: U.S. 'Reaching the Limits of Our Patience' with Pakistan Terror Safe Havens", CBS News, June 7, 2012. As of July 17, 2012, at http://

www.cbsnews.com/8301-503543_162-57448784-503543/ leon-panetta-u.s--reaching-the-limits-of-our-patience-with-pakistan-terror-safe-havens/

Bhasin, Avtar Singh (ed.), *India's Foreign Relations, 2007: Part I* (New Delhi: Ministry of External Affairs and Geetika Publishers, 2008).

———, (ed.), *India's Foreign Relations, 2008: Part I* (New Delhi: Ministry of External Affairs and Geetika Publishers, 2009).

"Biography", Office of the President, Islamic Republic of Afghanistan, undated. As of June 15, 2012, at http://president.gov.af/en/Page/1043

Blackwill, Robert D., "The Future of US-India Relations", speech hosted by the Confederation of Indian Industries, New Delhi, May 5, 2009. As of June 19, 2012, at http://www.aspenindia.org/outreach/pdf/Blackwill_speech_May_05_2009.pdf

Blair, Dennis, Director of National Intelligence, "Annual Threat Assessment of the US Intelligence Community for the Senate Select Committee on Intelligence", February 2, 2010. As of June 18, 2012, at http://www.dni.gov/testimonies/20100202_testimony.pdf

Blake, Robert O. Jr., Assistant Secretary, Bureau of South and Central Asian Affairs, U.S. Department of State, "The Obama Administration's Priorities in South and Central Asia, Remarks, Houston, Texas, January 19, 2011a. As of June 15, 2012, at http://www.state.gov/p/sca/rls/rmks/2011/155002.htm

———, Testimony before the U.S. House of Representatives Committee on Foreign Affairs, Subcommittee on the Middle East and South Asia, April 5, 2011b. As of June 18, 2012, at http://foreignaffairs.house.gov/112/65627.pdf

———, "Looking Ahead: U.S.–India Strategic Relations and the Transpacific Century", Remarks, National Bureau of Asian Research, Washington, DC, September 28, 2011c. As of June 18, 2012, at http://www.state.gov/p/sca/rls/rmks/2011/174139.htm

Blanchard, Christopher M., *Afghanistan: Narcotics and U.S. Policy* (Washington, DC: Congressional Research Service, RL32686, August 12, 2009).

Bodansky, Yossef, *Islamabad's Road Warriors* (Houston, Texas: Freeman Center for Strategic Studies, 1995).

Bokhari, Farhan, "With U.S. Military Aid Cut, Pakistan Eyes China", CBS News, July 10, 2011. As of June 19, 2012, at http://www.cbsnews.com/8301-503543_162-20078219-503543.html

Brennan, John O., Assistant to the President for Homeland Security and Counterterrorism, "The Ethics and Efficacy of the President's Counterterrorism Strategy", Remarks, Woodrow Wilson Center, Washington, DC, April 30, 2012. As of June 19, 2012, at http://www.wilsoncenter.org/event/the-efficacy-and-ethics-us-counterterrorism-strategy

"Brennan: Post-9/11, U.S. Has 'Right Balance' Between Civil Liberties, Security", *PBS Newshour*, September 7, 2011. As of June 19, 2012, at http://www.pbs.org/newshour/bb/politics/july-dec11/johnbrennan_09-07.html

Brummitt, Chris, "NATO Invites Pakistan to Summit in Chicago", Associated Press, May 15, 2012.

Bumiller, Elisabeth, and Jane Perlez, "Pakistan's Spies Linked to Raid on US Embassy", *Boston Globe*, September 23, 2011. As of June 18, 2012, at http://www.bostonglobe.com/news/world/2011/09/22/pakistan-aided-embassy-strike-mullen-says/ysOg2WMdqrO1Ge4jvm5mZJ/story.html

———, "The Bonn Conference: Can Afghanistan Be Saved Without Pakistan on Board?", *Time*, December 5, 2011. As of June 18, 2012, at http://world.time.com/2011/12/05/the-bonn-conference-can-afghanistan-be-saved-without-pakistan-on-board/

Tharoor, Shashi, "Hooray for Bollywood: India's 'Soft Power", *Taipei Times*, January 7, 2008. As of June 15, 2012, at http://www.taipeitimes.com/News/editorials/archives/2008/01/07/2003396110

Transparency International, *Corruption Perceptions Index 2011*, 2011. As of June 18, 2012, at http://transparency.org/whatwedo/pub/corruption_perceptions_index_2011

"Turkmenistan-Afghanistan-Pakistan-India Gas Pipeline: South Asia's Key Project", *PetroMin Pipeliner*, April-June 2011. As of June 14, 2012, at http://www.pm-pipeliner.safan.com/mag/ppl0411/r06.pdf

"U.S. AfPak Envoy Backs Indian Investment in Afghanistan, Strategic Pact", Indo-Asian News Service, October 12, 2011.

US Agency for International Development, "Energy in Pakistan", Working Paper, April 2011a. As of June 19, 2012, at http://transition.usaid.gov/pk/docs/sectors/Energy_Working_Paper.pdf

———, "Pakistan: Energy Program", September 2011b. As of June 19, 2012, at http://transition.usaid.gov/pk/sectors/energy/docs/en_factsheet.pdf

US Department of State, "U.S.–India Strategic Dialogue Joint Statement", Media Note, June 3, 2010. As of June 18, 2012, at http://www.state.gov/r/pa/prs/ps/2010/06/142645.htm

US Energy Information Administration, "Pakistan: Country Analysis Brief," June 30, 2010a.

———, "India: Country Analysis Brief", August 2010b.

———, "India", Washington DC, Country Analysis Brief, November 21, 2011. As of June 19, 2012, at http://www.eia.gov/EMEU/cabs/India/pdf.pdf

"U.S. Set to Ignore Pakistan, Afghanistan in Taliban Talks", *Press TV*, February 10, 2012. As of June 18, 2012, at http://www.presstv.ir/detail/226023.html

"U.S. Suspends $800 Million in Aid to Pakistan", NPR, July 10, 2011. As of June 14, 2012, at http://www.npr.org/2011/07/10/137746664/u-s-to-suspend-800-million-in-aid-to-pakistan

Verma, Arjun, and Teresita Schaffer, "A Difficult Road Ahead: India's Policy on Afghanistan", *South Asia Monitor*, no. 144, August 1, 2010. As of June 15, 2012, at http://csis.org/files/publication/SAM_144.pdf

Wafa, Abdul Waheed, and Alan Cowell, "Suicide Car Blast Kills 41 in Afghan Capital", *New York Times*, July 8, 2008. As of June 18, 2012, at http://www.nytimes.com/2008/07/08/world/asia/08afghanistan.html

Waldman, Matt, "The Sun in the Sky: The Relationship Between Pakistan's ISI and Afghan Insurgents", London: London School of Economics and Political Science, Crisis States Research Centre, Working Paper 18, 2010.

Warrick, Joby, and Karen DeYoung, "CIA Helped India, Pakistan Share Secrets in Probe of Mumbai Siege", *Washington Post*, February 16, 2009. As of June 25, 2012, at http://www.washingtonpost.com/wp-dyn/content/article/2009/02/15/AR2009021501957.html

Waslekar, Sundeep, Leena Pillai, and Shabnam Siddiqui, "The Future of Pakistan", Strategic Foresight Group, Mumbai, 2002.

Wax, Emily, "India's Eager Courtship of Afghanistan Comes at a Steep Price", *Washington Post*, April 3, 2010. As of June 15, 2012, at http://www.washingtonpost.com/wp-dyn/content/article/2010/04/02/AR2010040204313.html

"We Have Only Four Consulates in Afghanistan, Exactly the Same Number We Had Earlier", *Rediff News*, February 26, 2009. As of June 15, 2012, at http://specials.rediff.com/news/2009/feb/26sld5-interview-with-indias-afghan-envoy-jayant-prasad.htm

Weinbaum, Marvin G., and Jonathan B. Harder, "Pakistan's Afghan Policies and Their Consequences", *Contemporary South Asia*, vol. 16, no. 1, 2008, pp. 25-38.

Weinbaum, Marvin G., and Haseeb Humayoon, "The Intertwined Destinies of Afghanistan and Pakistan", in J. Alexander Thier (ed.), *The Future of Afghanistan* (Washington, DC: U.S. Institute of Peace, 2009), pp. 93-104.

"What Is Bollywood?" *Newsround*, undated. As of June 15, 2012, at http://news.bbc.co.uk/cbbcnews/hi/find_out/guides/2003/bollywood/newsid_2683000/2683799.stm

White House, "Joint Statement by President Obama and Prime Minister Singh of India", Press Release, November 8, 2010. As of June 18, 2012, at http://www.whitehouse.gov/the-press-office/2010/11/08/joint-statement-president-obama-and-prime-minister-singh-india

"White Paper of the Interagency Policy Group's Report on U.S. Policy Toward Afghanistan and Pakistan", undated. As of June 18, 2012, at http://www.whitehouse.gov/assets/documents/Afghanistan-Pakistan_White_Paper.pdf

Yardley, Jim, "Indians Host Clinton While Also Wooing Iran", *New York Times*, May 8, 2012. As of June 19, 2012, at http://www.nytimes.com/2012/05/09/world/asia/india-and-iran-keep-economic-relations-despite-us-nudge.html?pagewanted=all

Younossi, Obaid, Peter Dahl Thruelsen, Jonathan Vaccaro, Jerry M. Sollinger, and Brian Grady, *The Long March: Building an Afghan National Army* (Santa Monica, CA: RAND Corporation, MG-845-RDCC/ OSD, 2009). As of June 18, 2012, at http://www.rand.org/pubs/monographs/MG845.html

Zoellick, Robert B., "Afghanistan's Biggest Need: A Flourishing Economy", *Washington Post*, July 22, 2011. As of June 18, 2012, at http://www.washingtonpost.com/opinions/afghanistans-biggest-need-a-flourishing-economy/2011/07/19/gIQAGNMIUI_story.html

5. Afghanistan: Issues and Challenges in Taliban Era

Rajkumar Singh

First Inning of Taliban and Afghan Ethnicity

From the year 1996 to 2001 the Taliban ruled a large part, about three-quarters of Afghanistan's land, and implemented a strict type of Sharia or Islamic law in the country and transferred the capital of Afghanistan to Kandahar of the new Islamic Emirate of Afghanistan, recognised only by three nations—Pakistan, Saudi Arabia and United Arab Emirates. As the country had suffered a lot on account of militancy and gang war in the last two decades, the role of international charitable and development organisations became most significant in war-torn territories to look after the needs of the masses. In this period the most affected portion of the government was humanitarian aid, supply of food, employment, reconstruction, and other services. The rule of the Taliban and its allies was responsible for massacre of Afghan civilians as they conducted the policy of scorched earth, burnt vast areas of fertile land and destroyed tens of thousands of homes, banned hobbies, but totally failed to check violence and ongoing gang/group wars on Afghanistan soil. All international agencies, including the United Nations Organisation reported against the misrule and anti-humanitarian attitude of the Taliban rule for which the Government of Pakistan was also responsible for extending all help—moral, material, financial, logistical and military support. The then regime of Afghanistan, according to several international sources, took help of Pakistani nationals, Pakistani trained fighters, and Al Qaeda militants to fight against the anti-Taliban forces in the country.

In post-9/11 phase when it became clear that Osama bin Laden, the Al Qaeda chief, was the mastermind of this mishappening, and he is hiding in Afghanistan, the United States of America exerted pressure on the Taliban to hand over the culprit to which the latter refused. As a result, America began a decisive war against the terror groups in Afghanistan in October 2001, along with joint forces of the UK, Canada, and other NATO member countries. Since then it is continuing till date. Apart from internal struggle among different militia groups in the country, the main fight remained between Taliban forces and the US-led forces and security forces of Afghan government. Although efforts for peace in Afghanistan are continuing for the last one decade, and even parties concerned have a concluded agreement in 2016 and 2020, due to non-implementation of certain conditions by them they proved futile and peace continued to a daunting task for all. However, the peace exercises made it amply clear that in today's context the Taliban has become the number one force or party in the Afghan peace process which no one can deny or overlook.

The Islamic Republic of Afghanistan is a mountainous landlocked country of Central and South Asia bordered by Pakistan to the east and south, Iran to the west, Turkmenistan, Uzbekistan and Tajikistan to the north and China to the northeast. In modern times, after the Third Anglo-Afghan War of 1919 the country became free and adopted monarchy under Amanullah Khan. In the year 1973 Zahir Shah was overthrown and a short-lived republic was born which followed the establishment of a socialist state after a second coup in 1978. As of today, in 2021, the population of Afghanistan is around 37,466,414 which includes roughly 3 million Afghan citizens living as refugees in both Pakistan and Iran. It's a multi-ethnic society which includes Pashtun 38.5%, Tajik 21.3%, Hazara 24.5%, Uzbek 6%, Aimak 3.2%, Turkmen 1.2%, Baloch 0.5% and others, such as Pashai, Nuristani, Arab, Brahui, Pamiri and Gujjar, 4.9%. Of the total populations, approximately 46% is under 15 years of age; 74% of all Afghans live in rural areas; while about 26% of the population is urban. There are two important languages—Pashto and Dari, popularly known and widely spoken in most parts of the country, and Uzbek and Turkmen are smaller languages used in some parts of the north. As a result, multilingualism is common throughout the country especially in major cities. Islam is the single dominant religion followed by more than 99% of Afghan citizens; 89.7% of the population practise Sunni Islam and belong to Hanafi Islamic law school, while 10% to 15% belong to Shia Islam and follow Twelver branch. A very thin population, about 0.3%, also practise Sikhism and Hinduism. Recently, alike other nations of the world, a nationwide e-ID programme has been launched to know the exact figures about the size and composition of ethnicity in the country, although Article 4 of the present constitution of the country mentions 14 ethnic groups by names.

Although no official census has been done in the country since 1979, the total number of Pashtuns is estimated to be around 63 million in Afghanistan, historically known as Iranian ethnic group, native to Central and South Asia, speaking the group's language Pashto, but this group of Afghanistan also use the Dari, a dialect of Persian, as a second language. Those in the Indian subcontinent use Hindi-Urdu as a second language and most of them reside in southern Afghanistan and northwestern Pakistan, occasionally also referred to as Pashtunistan. Their area is mostly located south of the river Amu Darya in Afghanistan and west of the Indus River in Pakistan, comprising the Khyber Pakhtunkhwa and northern Baluchistan. The history of modern Afghans is related back to the regime of Delhi Sultanate, particularly the Hotak dynasty and Durrani Empire. In fact, Ahmad Shah Durrani was a military commander under Nader Shah who created the last Afghan empire that covered most part of today's Afghanistan, Pakistan, Kashmir, Indian Punjab as well as the Kohistan and Khorasan province of Iran. The decline of the Durrani dynasty was succeeded by Barakzai dynasty around 1826 to 1973 when Zahir Shah took the reins of administration. The end of monarchy and rule of President Daoud Khan, who was assassinated in 1978, and Soviet intervention in December 1979, paved the way for proxy war in the region. By that time Pakistan became active and began recruiting Mujahideen guerrilla for a warfare against the Democratic Republic of Afghanistan. The Mujahideen were a pro-Islamic guerrilla group engaged in jihad to fight on behalf of Islam/Allah, or the Islamic community. Although, the

Soviet intervention was justified in order to defeat a rising insurgency in the country, the Mujahideen were mainly funded by the United States of America, Saudi Arabia, China and others, and comprised some Pashtun commanders like Gulbuddin Hekmatyar and Jalaluddin Haqqani.

With the Soviet intervention in Afghanistan, millions of Pashtuns decided to flee the country and settled in Afghan diaspora in Pakistan and Iran. Some of them proceeded to North America, the European Union, the Middle East, Australia and other parts of the world. The new developments altered the balance of power in Afghanistan where Pashtuns were historically dominant. The emergence of new well-organised armed groups comprising Tajiks, Uzbeks and Hazaras, combined with fragmented Pashtuns, reduced the influence of earlier Pashtuns and, thus, in both groups, Taliban and the Northern Alliance, Pashtuns were part and parcel who were fighting against each other in the country. The two main Pashtuns—Gulbuddin Hekmatyar and Haqqani—were considered as top leadership of the Taliban while Abdullah and Abdul Qadir brothers were sided with Northern Alliance and fighting against the Taliban. If one is not wrong Northern Alliance is a partner of Afghan government, taking all help from the United States of America. When the Taliban regime was ousted in 2001 with the help of America-led war in Afghanistan, it was replaced by Karzai administration, followed by Ghani reign in succession. Even today Pashtuns are in dominant position in both groups and they are not only playing an important role in South Asia but also in Central Asia and the Middle East. In addition, there are so many noted Pashtun personalities of India and Pakistan who have adopted non-Pashtun culture and learned the languages, such as Urdu, Punjabi and Hindko.

At large, the Pashtuns across the region and the globe adhere to Pashtunwali codes and are recognised by the culture, not by religion. They are not homogeneous strictly in religious terms, although the overwhelming majority of them belong to Sunni sect with a tiny Shia community. Alike religion, speaking Pashto language is not an essential criterion of being a Pashtun, but only patrilineal definition is applied everywhere equally according to which only those who have a Pashtun father are Pashtun. There are so many other groups who claim to be Pashtun but do not speak

Pashto language and are considered overlapping groups, having different geographical location and mother tongue. Likewise, the Pathans of India have lost both—language and ways of their ancestors but trace out Pashtun origin and ethnic heritage.

Second Inning of Taliban Rule

August 15, 2021, now became a red-letter day in the history of modern Afghanistan because the Taliban—a militant turned political group—in a series of capture/victory ultimately occupied Kabul, the capital of Afghanistan and compelled an elected President of the country to take shelter in a neighbouring nation, with thousands of others who disliked the earlier regime of the Taliban between 1996 and 2001. It was a black day for the people across the world who cherish and strive for love, peace, security, modernity, freedom, human rights and for all our social and individual desires. For the first time, this group was formed in the early 1990s as Afghan Mujahideen or Islamic guerilla fighters, committed to following the rules of Shariat in toto; the same people or group gave a neck-to-neck fight to the Soviet army between 1979 and 1989 and pushed them back to the Kremlin; however, this time they have defeated the force and influence of the United States of America who created and prepared them in the 1980s to fight against the Soviet Union when the Cold War between the two Superpowers was in active mode. Followed by years of civil war in post-Soviet withdrawal phase, the Taliban for the first time took over the reins of administration in 1996 overthrowing President Burhanuddin Rabbani, an ethnic Tajik whom they viewed as anti-Pashtun and corrupt, and continued for the next five years till 2001. It was a rule of a harsh brand of justice drawn from the Pashtuns' pre-Islamic code and interpretation of Sharia coloured by the austere Wahhabi doctrines of the madrasas which cast a long dark shadow on societal politics of Afghanistan. This time the Taliban have become stronger and more powerful on all counts in comparison to the regime it assumed 20 years ago. Naturally people of the globe, region and particularly of the country are fearful and suspicious about the further actions and motives of the rulers who are not foreigners but far away from the norms of modern governance.

The first term of the Taliban is known as the Islamic Emirate of Afghanistan in which it held power roughly over three-quarters of the country and strictly enforced Islamic laws under the leadership of Mohammed Omar for the whole period. It was a phase of massacre of Afghan civilians; denial of food supplies given by the United Nations to the starving people of Afghanistan; burning vast areas of fertile land; banning of media activities, including painting, in particular; photography and movies that showed people leaving things. In particular, their regime was wholly negative for girl children and women who were forced to live under severe inhuman and painful situations. They are not allowed to go to school for education and jobs except for health-care services where male doctors were prevented from seeing women. Women were not allowed to go outside the house alone but only with a male member and bearing burqa at all times when in public. In the sphere of religion, the rule of the Taliban was considered as anti-ethnic, anti-minority and anti-culture; as per a UN report, they discriminated against them at large and destroyed several historical monuments and buildings/temples of ancestral memory. They declared religious and cultural differences with the West and at the same time a war between the West and Islam. As most of the Taliban belong to Pashtun tribal origin, ideologically, it was an innovative form of Sharia based on Deobandi fundamentalism combined with militant Islamism along with Pashtun social and cultural norms known as Pashtunwali. In addition, there were several rules and practices strictly imposed on non-Pashtun ethnic groups which reminded us of the laws of Middle-Ages history, however, these all were implemented wholly in cities of Afghanistan while rural areas remained partially affected by the new waves of the Taliban.

In the first regime of Taliban rule in Afghanistan most decisions were made on the Pashtun tribal jirga believed to be modelled on the early Islamic model. One scholar, Rashid had described the rule as a secret society run by Kandaharis, mysterious, secretive, and dictatorial. In fact, the Taliban did not believe in elections; as its spokesman said, the Sharia does not allow politics or political parties, no salary but only food, clothes, shoes, and weapons to officers and soldiers, as we want citizens to lead a life the Prophet lived 1,400 years ago, and our aim is to recreate that life and times for the people of Afghanistan. But after consulting jirga, the Taliban's leader declared himself as 'Amir al-Mu'minin' or Commander of the Faithful, and instead of elections, leaders' legitimacy came from the oath of allegiance, in imitation of the Prophet and the first four Caliphs. In this way, by converting himself as a messenger of the Faithful, Mullah Mohammed Omar became all in all in Talibanic administration for whom no consultation was required and government will implement only those decisions he agreed upon. Alike the rule of early Muslim governance, there was a wide lack of state institutions, or a methodology for command and control and no press release, policy statement, or press conference and people in general remained unaware about their leaders' doings. In the context, it is also to be noted that the first government of the Taliban got diplomatic recognition of only four countries which include Pakistan, the United Arab Emirates, Turkmenistan, and Saudi Arabia who also helped them with substantial aid while other states of the globe continued to recognise the Islamic State of Afghanistan.

In comparison with the earlier capture of power by the Taliban, in mid-August 2021 it has multiplied the threat several times as its power, arms, ammunition with an increased number of fighters as well as open support and help of Pakistan and China clearly indicated a distinct shift in regional and global balance of power along with inter-state relations among the nations of Asia at large, and South Asia in particular. This time, the Taliban has fought perhaps the longest war in the history of warfare almost continuously from 2001 to 2021 against a Superpower with whom was the active support of NATO and other allies. It proved the most devastating struggle so far of the region in which some 47,000 civilians died along with 73,000 Afghan troops and police forces since 2007 when chances of coming peace were destroyed and both sides intensified the war to win over the other side decisively. With this ominous regional development all hopes of establishing peace in Afghanistan and providing security to its citizens have been belied once again, and the country along with the region have been pushed towards an uncertain future about which no one can predict anything at this juncture.

Today, the fate Afghanistan, from where the US-led forces of the NATO countries are on the point of withdrawal, is hanging in the balance and all things will be clear from the arrangements made for the country thereafter. Despite degradation of democracy and abuse of human rights at large even by pro-government elements, the nation has gained/protected a lot in these spheres and now the protection of these values through peace settlements has become a haunting problem for all concerned. In the context, in no way the Taliban is committed to these issues and made it clear on several occasions that if it comes to power it will rule the country as per Islamic laws, but never detailed its vision or plan of ruling the country after withdrawal of foreign forces from the country. On several occasions the Taliban deputy political leader Ghani Baradar in September 2020, February 2021 and in June 2021, has made it clear that the Taliban wanted an independent, sovereign, united developed and free Afghanistan, and added that his group is committed to protect certain rights with conditions as mentioned in the Islamic laws and freedom of speech within the framework of Islamic principles and national interests; while in a latest statement its spokesman threatened that if the goal of Islamic law is not reached, it will be compelled to continue the war to achieve that goal.

Basics of Taliban Rule and Regional Challenges

Sharia laws are traditional Islamic laws to lead a life based on the Quran and the Hadith derived from the sayings and actions of the Prophet Muhammad, literally mean "the way" or "path" in Arabic, from where most Muslims get their moral direction about their conduct, prayer and treatment of others, including family members. While some countries of the world follow the Sharia rules of traditional Islam in toto, others use their modern interpretations done by religious scholars, jurists and modern courts influenced by Western thought and practices of jurisprudence. In today's life it is very difficult, and sometimes inhuman, to obey the rules of traditional faith, made for the society which existed, if not a thousand, a hundred years ago, when all parameters of life have changed in essence. The classical Sharia is a whole set and dealt with aspects of public and private life, including religious rituals, family life, business, crimes, and warfare, and while some laws of Sharia can be accepted as usual, others are better understood as rules for living life in accordance with God's will. In most Muslim countries only a small part of the Sharia laws has been implemented as a token, and other practices of their law are influenced by Western views of jurisprudence which respect human rights, gender equality, and freedom of speech; but, in general, they all have a poor opinion about women, especially for those who are captured in wars and considered as war lootings. Most Muslim countries went far away from Sharia because they wanted to be more powerful, and hence took European state models along with other traits of modernity. In many cases where Muslim states were colonised by the Europeans, they forced them to abandon several parts of Sharia law and follow European laws instead for a long time.

Originally, Sharia in Islam is considered as the revealed law of God which cannot be altered at any cost, and rests on five sources: (a) Qur'an, which they believed to be revealed by God to Muhammad, (b) the actions and words of Muhammad, which are called Sunnah and preserved in collection called Hadith, (c) on consensus, when all legal experts agree, and (d) a legal reasoning by analogy. The whole set of Sharia laws have been classified in several parts/actions from the viewpoints of their significance: (a) actions that one must perform, (b) recommended actions, (c) action that is allowed, (d) action that is despised, and (e) action that is prohibited. Of these all the acts have been divided in two branches—acts of worship and human interaction. Of them, worship is viewed as compulsory and called the pillars of Islam, which include: (a) affirmation, the concept that there is no God except Allah and Muhammad is his messenger, (b) prayer, five times a day, (c) fasting during Ramadan, (d) charity or Zakat, and (e) pilgrimage to Mecca or Haj. Alike these there are laws of dietary, sacrifice, family life, and crime and punishment. In crime and punishment there are offences which found a place in Quran and considered as violating 'claims of God' and have fixed punishments. In the second category are offences which are against persons, such as murder and wounding, and call for a punishment in proportion to the crime or payment of compensation, while punishments in other forbidden behaviour are fixed by a Muslim judge using his discretion. Although there are differences among scholars and jurists about the crimes which come under 'hudud' category, they normally include theft, highway robbery, Zina or sex with forbidden partners, falsely accusing someone of Zina, and drinking alcohol. The prescribed punishment for these crimes ranges from 80 lashes to death. As per hudud, these crimes require other difficult formalities and as such people often ignore their implementation, but historically, the system of Qisas remained in practice which include the punishment with 'counteraction' meaning a life for life, an eye for an eye along with consideration of one's social status.

The initial phase of Sharia laws that prevailed in the world was not so harsh and commonly considered as moderate for non-Muslims living under the rule where criminal cases were handled in mazalim courts, controlled by ruler's council. At the time mazalim courts were hoped to follow "the spirit of Sharia" where the Qadis and muftis were also present to ensure the implementation of Sharia. In particular, the mazalim courts also handled the complaints against government officials which were not decided by qadi courts in proper way, while local crimes or low-level crimes were settled by local police and market inspectors according to local customs, without any concern for Sharia. Such rules were good also for non-Muslims who lived under the regime because they were allowed to follow their own laws until or unless there was any dispute between two religious communities; while hearing those cases preference was given to non-Muslims, in the supposition that the Sharia is the reflection of the divine who desires to defend the weak against the powerful. The further developments of Sharia were registered in the 20th and 21st centuries because of demographic changes that took place in the nation's life.

With the passage of time several Muslim countries adopted western ways in their legal system; many people regarded their action as oppressive, corrupt, and ineffective, leading to a general disappointment in Muslim countries across the globe. As this thinking went on increasing, nations began to rethink their strategy and finally decided in favour of Sharia laws where they could find solutions for all problems. On the other hand, a large group of conservative people want use of the traditional methods in handling the crimes with the help of hudud punishment. In the light of recent trends, several countries including Iran and Sudan adopted the hudud system of punishment, but the Supreme Court of the country rarely approved harsher punishments, while in Pakistan and Nigeria, the apex court never accepts Sharia laws in delivering crime judgments. In the whole Muslim world, Saudi Arabia is the single Muslim country who has applied Sharia laws in different spheres and never codified its separate laws. Its court judges always follow Sharia laws while delivering crime judgments, but apply only the classical principle which says that hudud punishments should be avoided. The Taliban, the present ruler of Afghanistan, which captured power by force, has also avowed to follow the Sharia rules and the reason South Asia is fearful about its nefarious motives and designs.

For more than four decades the country Afghanistan has been a playground for super and regional powers, and is on the verge of being free from foreign forces on its soil since October 7, 2001, when the United States launched a decisive war against terrorism especially in search of Osama bin Laden, the Al Qaeda chief. The President duo of America- Donald Trump and Joe Biden have reiterated US policy to withdraw its forces from Afghanistan which has already begun and likely to be completed by September 11, 2021, the 20th anniversary of Washington's longest war on foreign soil. During the entire period of war against terror fought by Afghan security forces backed by American-led forces of NATO countries, who also got the moral support of India, New Delhi has helped Afghanistan a lot in the construction and restructuring of the country's infrastructures that ultimately pave the way for making a good understanding among America, Afghanistan and India, who all want a fairly elected/democratic government in post-withdrawal Kabul. Against this is the group which includes Pakistan, the Taliban, China and, recently Russia, with Islamabad in the role of team-leader, a leader who did not want there to be a pro-India government, and trying its level best to push the Taliban to the throne of Afghanistan to establish an Islamic State, and also perform as a puppet government of Pakistan. From the beginning, the Taliban has flourished under the shadow and substantial help of Pakistan, and consequently Islamabad wields a large amount of influence in the working of the Taliban. To a large extent, the Taliban is obliged to Pakistan but in no way is it opposed to India, while Pakistan is totally committed to an "India-mukt" Afghanistan. Its victory lies in the victory of the Taliban—either by electoral process or military might. In that kind of situation, the other group feared the return of the old Taliban rule between 1996 and 2001, a true disaster for democratic values.

Since February 29, 2020, when the United States signed an agreement with the Taliban and both sides committed to obey the conditions attached with it, the way for withdrawal of foreign forces from Afghanistan appeared clear and with it the stakeholders of Afghan politics began to ponder over the situation after their saying goodbye. In this short period India needs to reset its policy preferences in Kabul because the Taliban group after the agreement has emerged as a potent force of Afghan politics which nobody can deny. But New Delhi has continuously denied the importance of the Taliban also because it has remained on Pakistan's side and opposed to India. Indian development works and assets have always been targeted by the Haqqani group, a major faction of the Taliban. The fast-changing situations in Afghanistan demand from India to work with the Taliban, a terror New Delhi has avoided so far. It has to do with the increasing influence of Pakistan's Inter-Services Intelligence (ISI) which shares a link with the Haqqani group. In addition to these two, India also needs to be ready for the instability in Afghanistan after withdrawal of foreign forces. At this juncture, what India needs to do is: (a) to keep alive broader diplomatic engagement by appointing an envoy for the purpose who will be acquainted with the latest developments and also let the government know full detail; (b) to continue the training programme for the Afghan security forces along with other schemes of investments which will make the Afghan army strong enough to face the coming odds, and (c) need to broaden the negotiation base by involving Iran, Russia, China and other concerned powers to seek a common ground for the future of Afghanistan and commence diplomatic initiatives at its level. In other words, India should rely more on long-term strategies rather than focusing only on present.

Conclusion

To a large extent the future course of action to be decided by Pakistan depends on the development of Afghanistan, whether military might be going to be victorious under the Taliban and its allies or the democratic process, as both the systems are known to the public with benefits and side effects. Especially after the fall of the Taliban rule in December 2001 and signing of the Bonn Agreement, which provided for the political system of the country, and in the year 2004 a new constitution was implemented in Afghanistan, the people have enjoyed the fruits of a democratic regime; while the period between 1996 and 2001, the rule of the Taliban prevailed in the country, where administration was run by the Islamic laws or as per the guidance of Sharia,was considered a dark age in terms of democracy and human rights abuses. In opposition to India, Pakistan had done everything possible to get the Taliban back in the driving seat in Kabul, but the time has come now to arrange and manage the things in the right way to have the desired result. In addition, Pakistan has faced a lot of charges from Washington for not cooperating with America in its war against terror and made only false promises along with keeping the US in the dark and telling a lie. This is why Pakistan has distanced itself from the US and openly begun to speak against America and in favour of China and Russia recently. The contemporary scenario of Afghanistan is a test case for the Taliban's ability to rule over the country by making a number of arrangements in favour of the public good. The US has already accepted it as a potential power of Afghan politics and now is the turn of the Taliban and its allied forces to show the level of maturity and skill to the public and America as well.

6. The Graveyard of Empires: An Endless War in Afghanistan

Jay Maniyar

A Brief History of Afghanistan from Great Powers' Perspective

The Islamic Republic of Afghanistan is a geographically-challenging, politically-complex, and a relatively large land-locked nation which is located at the heart of the Central-South Asian axis in continental Asia. It is approximately 650,000 sq. km. in land area. The country has been presently rechristened the "Islamic Emirate of Afghanistan" owing to its audacious takeover by one of the world's most feared ideological-fanatical terrorist groups, the Taliban (Pashto for 'students'). Its new leader is Mullah Mohammed Hassan Akhund, a Taliban head (leader of the *Rehbari Shura*[1]), who assumed the mantle of 'President' in September 2021.[2] Akhund was a foreign minister in a previous Taliban regime and his appointment came as a surprise with respect to other notable Taliban heads. The former Afghan leader, Ashraf Ghani, was forced to escape to the United Arab Emirates (UAE) by helicopter as the Taliban took over the country in its entirety after having stepped up attacks and making their intentions clear in the past few months. Ghani, then, issued a sorry "explanation statement" expressing solidarity with his now-abandoned Afghan population during this new crisis.[3]

In the present day, Afghanistan is now all but bereft of the presence of any great power at all, let alone qualified Superpowers with certain characteristics. The exit of the United States of America (US, USA), following an agreement with the Taliban (through its Doha office) in mid-2021, spectacularly announced by the incumbent Democrat President Joe

Biden, resulted in an emboldened Taliban having overpowered the then ruling Ghani government in the space of a few days to quickly assume sovereign control of the war-torn country. In February 2020, the United States had agreed terms with the Taliban to bring everlasting peace to a virulent and collapsing Afghanistan.[4] Prior to the US exit, the Taliban had already occupied several strategic parts of Afghanistan with a traditional stronghold in its southern territory, which is known to be the origin of the extremist group from where it parachuted to the rest of the country in the mid-1990s. The present regime has brought Afghanistan "on the brink of economic collapse" with its leaders unbefitting of steering the country ahead and condemning its abject past of sustained economic failure to the history books.[5]

This Paper attempts to trace the history of foreign 'empires' in Afghanistan, their subsequent downfall, and the future of the country with respect to new players such as the People's Republic of China (PRC, China), the Russian Federation, and the Republic of India. Given the strategic proximity of the latter to the complicated geography of Afghanistan, the country may now be witness to a new era wherein those that are deeply interested in its affairs are all but a stone's throw away from it. The Paper will conclude that 'multipolarity', a tenet of international relations that attempts to explain the balance of power, will form the basis of external involvement in Afghanistan for several years to come.

Why Is Afghanistan Called the "Graveyard of Empires"?

In its historical past, Afghanistan is one of the oldest regions in the world to have nurtured a human habitat. It has been accompanied by civilisations aplenty on the way to having become a country in 1823 as the "Emirate of Afghanistan", a term conspicuously used even today to describe Afghanistan under Taliban rule (minus the name of the country itself). The Pakhtun/Pashtun peoples have come to be the prominent natives of the central-south Asian country. Several other tribes within the ambit of Islam, such as Tajiks, Hazaras, and Uzbeks, have also found place with a civilian government in Kabul having embraced the entirety of its vast land following the formalisation of the Westphalian Afghan nation in 1919. Its mountainous and complex terrains with their seemingly unsurpassable demeanour are described to be 'rugged' and 'uninhabitable', which has provided fertile grounds for extremist groups of all ilk to ply their trade.[6]

For several decades now, Afghanistan has come to be known as the "graveyard of empires", a eulogy nonetheless owing to the ludicrously massive gaps in the sheer strengths of the uninvited guest power in comparison to Afghanistan itself. The word 'empire' is a reference to an uber-powerful, leading, global nation-state which set foot in a terrain such as Afghanistan's for purposes of its core national security, an uncompromisable tenet which found itself threatened from thousands of kilometres away. During the early nineteenth century, Great Britain, while going about establishing its incomprehensibly evil empire in India, saw itself interested in the lands to the west of India. The Kingdom of *Caubul*, as Kabul and Afghanistan were then known, was visited by Monstuart Elphinstone, a Scottish national in the government of British India. The intention of Britain, at the time, was to prevent colonial advances in Afghanistan and to get to better know the region.[7] That said, Britain found Afghanistan to be a very lucrative destination for its aspirations of global colonialism through widespread invasions and establishments of harsh governing rules. The main aim of Britain in colonially governing Afghanistan was the preservation of linkages with the crown jewel in its empire, India. The last of the Anglo-Afghan wars that took place during Britain's colonialism in Afghanistan resulted in British eviction from the country. The Treaty of Gandamak was to mark the first phase of Afghan independence from rule by the British Empire. The Treaty,[8] however, was signed at the time to ensure British control of the strategic Khyber pass and link British India with the headquarters of the empire in London.

The Soviet Union was the succeeding Superpower which embarked upon the conquest of Afghanistan in the 1970s and was responsible for triggering an ensuing insurgency which morphed into what is known as the Taliban today, and is officially called the Islamic Emirate of Afghanistan. The Taliban was constructed and formalised as a group in September 1994 from having previously been operational as independent mercenaries posited against the Soviet invasion, who were called the *mujahideen* (holy warriors of Islam). After initial successes, the Soviet Union struggled in maintaining itself in Afghan lands and eventually exited the country. This also ran parallel to its own demise as a Superpower in 1991 with its final president, Mikhael Gorbachev, having given a historical televised address then.

Afghanistan—The Graveyard of Empires

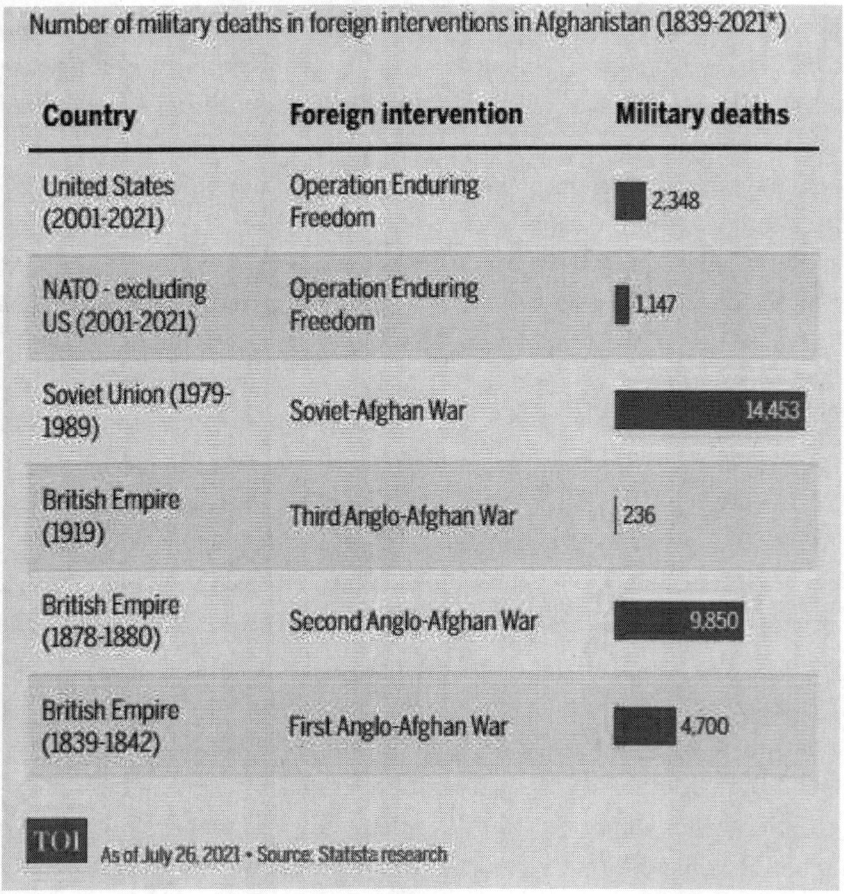
Number of military deaths in foreign interventions in Afghanistan (1839-2021*)

Country	Foreign intervention	Military deaths
United States (2001-2021)	Operation Enduring Freedom	2,348
NATO - excluding US (2001-2021)	Operation Enduring Freedom	1,147
Soviet Union (1979-1989)	Soviet-Afghan War	14,453
British Empire (1919)	Third Anglo-Afghan War	236
British Empire (1878-1880)	Second Anglo-Afghan War	9,850
British Empire (1839-1842)	First Anglo-Afghan War	4,700

TOI As of July 26, 2021 • Source: Statista research

Source: https://timesofindia.indiatimes.com/world/south-asia/explained-why-afghanistan-is-called-the-graveyard-of-empires/articleshow/84827451.cms

The USSR suffered 14,453 military deaths during its decade-long invasion (1979-1989), as per Statista research sourced from the *Times of*

India.[9] The Soviet Union, a communist Superpower, commenced its invasion on December 24, 1979 with it having ended in the Union's slow but steady demise during the late 1980s and early 1990s. The primary aim of this invasion was to support the communist movement in Afghanistan and ensure that anti-communist Islamists were exterminated or expelled from Kabul. The USSR, at its peak, was the harbinger of communist movements everywhere in the world, which marked the Cold War with its contemporary, the United States. It had succeeded in the challenging environs of Afghanistan by having endorsed a communist coup in the country in 1978. Post the invasion, the Soviets were able to reinstall a communist government in Kabul. The Soviet reign over Afghanistan came to an end in as classical terms as possible with the major Superpower that the USSR was, left frustrated and weakened by *mujahideen* fighters. Three Anglo-Afghan wars took place in centuries prior to the advent of the USSR in Afghanistan, with Britain having been involved to a great extent previously. Meanwhile, the United States itself was responsible for over two decades (2001-2021) of an asphyxiated conflict in Afghanistan, in which its own deployments suffered the losses of over 2,000 troops while civilian casualties witnessed an increase of 47% in 2021 from 2020, over the course of the period.[10] Utilisation of alternate modes of warfare such as high-tech unmanned aerial vehicles (UAVs, or drones), too, caused a lot of angst to the US as the invading Superpower appeared to admit to the deaths of scores of innocents caused in the attempt of destroying terrorism.

The exit (and the eventual disassembly) of the USSR, in the late 1980s, was followed by an absence of a superpower on Afghan land for a relatively long stretch of approximately a decade or so. This was also, incidentally, the period during which Afghanistan began to find itself at the centre of new geopolitical developments that were to do with the rise of terrorism and extremism aimed at civilian populations in the backdrop of strong political and ideological motivations. A tectonic shift was to follow in an Afghanistan coming together from the Soviet invasion that eventually shook its very foundations. During this time, Afghanistan also witnessed governments of an Islamic state, while it had been under a democratic regime, previously. The Islamic Emirate of Afghanistan emerged in 1996, headed by a fierce movement called the Taliban ('students') and its first leader in Mullah

Mohammed Omar (deceased, since 2013) and his influential second hand, Mullah Abdul Ghani Baradar (in control of the group's activities, missions, and plans as its de facto head). Since their establishment, the Taliban have grown leaps and bounds to become the most feared terrorist group in the world with the year 2018 having witnessed over 6,000 deaths solely due to the Taliban.[11] Afghanistan's recent history is also ignominiously characterised by two governments of the Taliban (the first led by Omar), who have since unleashed their despotic ways and means on a repressed population. Since 2004, Afghanistan had transitioned into an Islamic republic, the tenure of which came to an end with the recent takeover by the Taliban. Its last two presidents were Hamid Karzai and the now-overthrown Ashraf Ghani.

The United States spearheaded an alliance-driven entry, featuring partners of the North Atlantic Treaty Organisation NATO) such as France and Germany, into Afghanistan after having been left shell-shocked by the gruesome attacks on its mainland on September 11, 2001. Ever since the many waves of terror developed with the Islamist wave the most notable amongst them, the US has been a major target owing to its commitment to the global adoption of democracy as a governance system and towards the eradication of all elements of terror and extremism. The 9/11 attacks are known to be the worst ever carnage inflicted on a country resulting in the deaths of over 3,000 civilians, and one as the United States. The US landed in Afghanistan on October 7, 2001, exactly two years prior to its like-minded foray into Iraq in a bid to destroy Baghdad's secretly-developed nuclear arsenal and prevent nuclear weapons proliferation. Following bombing raids in Afghanistan with the help of NATO allies, the US commenced its two-decades-long stay and went on to establish a number of military bases in and around the country.

While the US' involvement in Afghanistan through Operation *Enduring Freedom* has featured a number of equally-participant western allies, the deaths of a large number of its troops in consonance with an instantly-changed American worldview of its national security (especially, in the wake of the 9/11 attacks) has largely ensured that the decades of 2001-2021 have been nothing more than a bold venture by a unilateral America. Previous US administrations committed themselves to concluding the War on Terror as soon as possible but were compelled to only provide more ground forces in the wake of escalating attacks and out-of-control situations. Presidents Barack Obama (2009-2016) and Donald Trump (2017-2020) upped troop counts to the tune of 30,000 and 3,000 respectively, during their reigns, while also unequivocally having stressed upon the damages caused by and the harms inflicted upon the United States in its dead-end missions in Afghanistan. It is even more disturbing that the War on Terror cost the United States, as per one estimate by the *Vox* platform, US$ 6 trillion and close to a million lives.[12]

The NATO deserves more than an honourable mention in this paper. The North Atlantic Treaty Organization, short for NATO, is an organisation of like-minded western democracies. It was founded in the immediate aftermath of the Second World War to prevent any form of threats akin to those that manifested as a result of Nazism and Fascism in the mid-twentieth century. It has been ever-present in Afghanistan all through America's years of operation, and has been more than an equal partner of the US in the country. The group from 1949 is notable for two major involvements: (a) provision of leadership for the United Nations' International Security Assistance Force (ISAF) since August 2003 till late 2014, and (b) its very own Resolute Support Mission (RSM) of 2015-present, which has also been undertaken to bolster the efforts of Afghan forces operating against the Taliban and its kind.[13] The NATO's cohesive and sustained strategy, via channels such as the ISAF and the RSM, demonstrates a "security empire" in the best interests of the Afghan people, as opposed to an empire from the "Great Game" times. As can be inferred from the above, the NATO's direct military involvement was also intended to eventually achieve the goal of Afghan forces being entirely in charge of the security of their nation, which is what is taking place in the present day. It is clear that NATO stretched its resources far beyond its primary area of operation by upping the ante in Afghanistan. NATO, perceivably, relies on an American security 'umbrella' and guidance to achieve its aims, goals, and objectives. In the present scenario, the Americans and NATO have adopted a policy of empowering local soldiers to eventually assume the mantle of responsibility in their country. American presence, in particular, has been devised and premised upon not just the empowerment of Afghan military forces but even the Afghan peoples as a whole. The country's rise and progress is seen as an imperative owing to the sorry state of affairs in regard to Afghan development and its deliberate destruction by a number of state and non-state actors within its boundaries and in its vicinity. American foreign policy avows the spread and adoption of forms of democracy as an ideal for the long term and the implementation of this aspect has found suitability in Afghanistan.

The US has even pondered a benevolent-minded occupation of Afghanistan in its entirety using its highly-advanced military as an instrument, with former Secretaries Colin Powell and Donald Rumsfeld advocating the possibility of American control of Afghanistan akin to its post-Second World War administration of Japan.[14] Before demitting office, Donald Trump had affirmed that the US could entirely destroy the terror infrastructure in Afghanistan but this would materialise at the cost of hundreds of thousands of Afghan lives in what he chose to describe as "endless wars" outside the national interest of America.[15] While an 'empire' might prove to be a derisory term in respect of the intent of the United States' involvement, the US has faced obstacles in plenty and these have forced the American hand to eventually abandon Afghanistan. To leave its future in the hands of its own leaders has, subsequently, proven to be an erroneous decision. The Taliban's iron-fisted rule is likely to continue ceaselessly were the US to not reconfigure its Afghanistan policy and deep-lying interests such as the annihilation of all of religion-based terrorism.

The complex geography and inhospitable terrains of Afghanistan have played a major role as an 'intangible force' behind the demise of superpowers amidst ever-spreading fundamentalism and extremism. It is not merely the religion-linked undertones that have resulted in a number of superpowers having failed decisively before freeing themselves from the worst. This is not to say that superpowers interested in Afghanistan aren't well geared themselves. Rash national interests coupled with impromptu decision-making and ultra-selfish resource wants leading to resource hunts have guided their ill-fated parlays into Afghanistan. Afghanistan, inclusive of entrenched mazes and unassailable terrains, also remains a comprehensive threat to the entire South Asian system as a whole. Recently, the Islamic State Khurasan province, or IS-K/ISIS-K, issued a threat that appeared to sound as an existential warning to Pakistan as a country.[16] The Islamic State's local Afghan province is provided immense moral and material support by the mothership of the Islamic State of Iraq and Syria (ISIS), which is based in the northern Middle Eastern region. The entire powerplay here, however, is immensely complicated because of the deep-state (the Pakistan Army and the ISI) situated within the background of Pakistan which remains inclined to utilise the IS-K as an asset for overpowering the Taliban or, at the very least, scuppering its interests and goals in Afghanistan.[17] Pakistan's own multidimensional intricacies with regard to home-grown terrorism and extremism offer Afghanistan no reprieve and their immediacy to each other is often characterised by porous borders and pointless relations. Afghanistan has not merely proven to be a "graveyard of empires" but even a cobweb of multiple players, state and non-state, with differing aims, ambitions, ideologies, interests, etc., and a determination to establish full control.

Wars Aplenty in Perennially Suffering Afghanistan

Afghanistan, fair to say, has been witness to a cocktail mix of what has been an extensive, prolonged, and long-drawn war between the United States in its sole capacity and a multitude of radical terrorist groups, wars between terrorist factions such as the Taliban and the Islamic State, and even (ongoing) wars within these very factions. Apart from the Islamic State's Khurasan branch, an organisation resident in the region for over half a decade now, the Taliban suffers from threats posed by a Pakistan determined to shape the regional status quo in its favour and determine the future of terrorism and extremism in its own inimitable ways. Even prior, everlasting turmoil has been a cause of the state's failure in rising as a developed power with the rise of the *mujahideen*. Fighting off superpowers has become a norm in the Afghan quagmire with both the complexities of its terrains and the determination of Islamists combining forces with relative ease. Afghanistan suffers from the tyranny of ravaged tribal groups which often results in escalated and prolonged violence detrimental to the country's nascent development regime. This is only further worsened by those very tribals now commanding the highest offices in the country, leading to bleak predictions of its future.

The United States-led War on Terror eventually found itself headquartered in Afghanistan for all intents and purposes. While neighbouring Pakistan was scrupulously known to provide the proverbial sanctuary for all sorts of terrorists (as also Talibs), Afghanistan remained the country that was most difficult to come to terms with owing to the scandalous nature of conflict on its territory. This was especially so in terms of what the War on Terror was seeking to accomplish as failures mounted, objectives grew and remain under- or unachieved, and financial distress accompanied the deaths of soldiers and civilians. A well-intentioned anti-terrorism campaign that was meant to limit the very word "war" in the "War on Terror" began to transform into a disturbing and devastating continuum of disastrous mini-conflicts with major repercussions. It is clear that the "War on Terror" followed from the 9/11 attacks on the United States' soil, which resulted in two returning theatres of conflict. Following on from the Soviet invasion of Afghanistan and the Gulf War involving tyrannical Iraq, these two countries were at the forefront of the US' "revenge" coupled with realising the aim of a terror-free world. While Presidents George W. Bush and Barack Obama spearheaded the American efforts in Afghanistan, the incumbent Joe Biden and his predecessor decided upon the withdrawal of America as a whole from Afghanistan. To those who assisted US efforts in the country, Washington promised them special immigrant visas and a residency in the United States' mainland.[18] The US remains self-admittedly defeated in the War on Terror but its overarching presence and exceptional military prowess will always be of concern to terrorist radicals and religiously-motivated extremists.

While it can be reasonably suggested that the might of nation-states, and superpowers especially so, cannot be compared with fringe radical elements, the sheer local acumen of the latter over the former cannot be disregarded. Failing superpowers have become a norm in geographically-vulnerable regions while minor groups have gone on to command complete control. A new method will have to be applied by interested countries in a 'region' such as Afghanistan owing to the manifest possibilities of not just ordinary but exorbitant failure in tough terrains amid rogue presences. It is obviously preferred that a win-win situation be pursued. However, with governments increasingly cosying up to the Taliban in search of an imperative peace tantamount to progress, prosperity, reform, and rise in Afghanistan, a cloud of unpredictability has engulfed the region as a whole. The poor state of Kabul's economy, too, poses as much concern as the severity of prolonged Talib rule in the country, and the rulers themselves have stated that they are keen on not repeating the mistakes of the previous regime, which was largely extremist and radical in its nature. As per Connor Keane, 60-70% of Taliban recruits, between the years 2001 and 2008, are attributed to having resulted from a lack of quality employment and dependable sources of income.[19] That said, their policy-driven actions seem to be much to the contrary with foreign currencies, including the US dollar, having recently been banned from circulation all over Afghanistan.[20]

Conclusion—Multipolarity Is Poised to Engulf Afghanistan

That Afghanistan has been described aptly as a territory where perpetual conflict has found a permanent home, involving one massive power such as the US or the erstwhile USSR, and now China, Russia, or India, pegged against a host of non-traditional adversaries, is not a misguided attribution in the least. These well-organised adversaries constitute a huge and an even more complicated challenge all the more so to the Afghan government and external, well-intentioned players because they themselves continue to differ in ideology even if united by a single, overarching religion in Islam. On-ground, they are inclined to compete for influence and territory with each other and this has proven to be an occurrence on a regular basis. This has led to more complications in the "War on Terror", which has gone on to become a "War of Terror". The War of Terror involves a chaotic blend of ideologically-similar but politically-differing terrorist groups, their radical subgroups and affiliates, and scrupulous agencies with a uniquely external dimension such as Pakistan's Inter-Services Intelligence (ISI). In fact, with the complicated demeanour of Afghanistan in the present day, events of turmoil and turbulence in the country may even be called a "War of and by Terror". This would be in reference to a large number of routine terrorist attacks causing widespread deaths and destruction, and resulting effectively in a dimensionally-different but still full-scale conflict above anything else. As far as mainstream terror was concerned, Kabul has been witness to major attacks such as end-August 2021 suicide bombing on the city's international airport by the Islamic State Khurasan province, which killed and injured scores of innocents.

With communist USSR eternally condemned to the history books and capitalist US (possibly, eternally, too, as far as direct, unilateral involvement is concerned) having packed its bags in a decision that appeared to be in the making for several years, the next in line to potentially be disgraced in Afghanistan's infamous "graveyard of empires" may be a series of relatively lesser but geostrategically-inclined powers such as China, Russia, and India. The latter all but lack in comparison to the former as far as the correlation of the term 'empire' to themselves is concerned as they are mainly developing countries aiming to rule the world in 2050. It does appear as if the "graveyard of empires" moniker will in itself be buried soon because of a new trajectory of external involvement in Afghanistan. This is because an assortment of new ideologically-different actors with common and urgent interests, near and about Afghanistan, do not appear to want to involve themselves as deeply as the USSR and the US, and don't need to, either.

Instead, what is being witnessed is a unique blend of self-interested geostrategies being played out in Afghanistan by many rising powers seeking to achieve streamlined objectives far lacking in comparison to the world's two sole superpowers of then and now. While multipolarity, as a concept of the balance of power in international relations, is often attributed to a region, a continent, or the world as a whole, its application in the Afghan framework appears to be suitable in the wake of its evolution as an Islamic country. What is even more intriguing in Afghanistan's current scenario is that the three new powers may not be seeking to promote any ideology or establish supreme control in Kabul but are more likely to add their own dimension(s) to the cocktail mix. For example, between them, China and India are involved in territorial disputes not too far from Afghanistan itself, thus adding further complexity to their respective forays into Afghanistan. It remains to be seen what the future holds for the country with a prolonged intervention by new powers.

Between them, China, India, and Russia appear to be three major but still rising powers, that profess to smaller geopolitical stakes in the turbulent affairs of Afghanistan as compared to the United States and its allies or erstwhile USSR. However, the implications of their respective rise will ensure that Afghanistan is also considered vitally and in a different manner to the perceptions of the US. Moreover, the distinct political systems of the three countries will result in different approaches by the triumvirate to Afghanistan's developments. For example, India is now all but compliant to the Taliban regime now decisive about Afghan affairs with India's Ambassador to Qatar, Dr. Deepak Mittal, having met with Taliban officials recently.[21] As can be evinced from the discussions in the meeting, it is apparent that India *does* see the Taliban as an existential threat, chiefly to Kashmir, and the safety and security of Indian nationals based in the country are uncompromisable. While the overarching theme remains the dangers of widespread, large-scale conflict and wars within the Afghan framework, vested interests such as the hunt for Afghanistan's rich resources (for example, rare earths and minerals such as iron, copper, and lithium) will prove that there indeed may be new developments similar to the "Great Game" of the nineteenth century between Great Britain and the Russian Empire. The ensuing months and years, and decades, will prove to be extremely challenging for the ordinary Afghan people to negotiate and this may result in the further downfall of their nation.

As opposed to subregional mini- or multilateralism which would result in a rational handling of the many prevailing issues of Afghanistan, multipolarity is now highly likely to engulf the consequential Islamic country. Strategically-located Afghanistan is finding itself in a unique situation involving a number of emerging powers, which further compounds the chaos and confusion well embedded within its borders since time immemorial. This could unleash a new cooperative-developmental era involving the might of the new powers, or possibly even further worsen Kabul's position in the fragile geopolitics of Central-South Asia. While other countries with an improving security mettle, such as Japan, may also be interested in attempting to shape the Afghan status quo, the three major powers named above in consonance with a democratic government in Kabul are best placed to replace a dithering West. The uniquely-Afghan moniker—"graveyard of empires"—could, thus, yet resurface with new victims waiting to be consumed amidst the monstrosity of its unalterable geographical terrains.

Notes

1. "Mullah Hassan to head proposed Taliban govt in Afghanistan with Baradar as his deputy: Report", last modified September 7, 2021, *India Today*, accessed on September 7, 2021, at https://www.indiatoday.in/world/story/afghanistan-taliban-leadership-new-govt-mullah-hassan-baradar-yaqoob-haqqani-1850261-2021-09-07
2. "Profile: Mohammed Hasan Akhund, the head of Taliban government", last modified September 7, 2021, *Al Jazeera*, accessed on November 7, 2021, at https://www.aljazeera.com/news/2021/9/7/profile-mohammad-hassan-akhund-the-head-of-taliban-government
3. "Ashraf Ghani", last modified September 9, 2021, CNBC, accessed on November 7, 2021, at https://www.cnbc.com/2021/09/09/ashraf-ghani-afghanistan-ex-president-issues-explanation-after-fleeing.html
4. "Joint Declaration between the Islamic Republic of Afghanistan and the United States of America for bringing peace to Afghanistan", last modified February 29, 2020, US Department of State, accessed on November 6, 2021, at https://www.state.gov/wp-content/uploads/2020/02/02.29.20-US-Afghanistan-Joint-Declaration.pdf
5. "Afghanistan's economy is on the brink of collapse", last modified October 25, 2021, Yahoo News, accessed on November 6, 2021, at https://news.yahoo.com/afghanistans-economy-brink-collapse-233002164.html
6. G. S. Goraya, *The Great Game—Afghanistan, British India, and the Hundred Year War for India's Northern Frontier* (ebook, Amazon Kindle), p. 13.
7. Goraya, *The Great Game*, p. 35.
8 "Treaty of Gandamak", *Encyclopedia Britannica*, accessed on November 6, 2021, at https://www.britannica.com/topic/Treaty-of-Gandamak
9. "Explained: Why Afghanistan is called the graveyard of empires", last modified July 28, 2021, *Times of India*, accessed on October 25, 2021, at https://timesofindia.indiatimes.com/world/south-asia/explained-why-afghanistan-is-called-the-graveyard-of-empires/articleshow/84827451.cms
10. "Civilian casualties set to hit unprecedented highs in 2021 unless urgent action to stem violence—UN Report", last modified July 26, 2021, United Nations Assistance Mission in Afghanistan, accessed on November 6, 2021, at

https://unama.unmissions.org/civilian-casualties-set-hit-unprecedented-highs-2021-unless-urgent-action-stem-violence-%E2%80%93-un-report

11. "ISIL is No Longer the World's Deadliest Terror Group", *Vision of Humanity*, accessed on November 7, 2021, at https://www.visionofhumanity.org/isil-is-no-longer-the-worlds-deadliest-terrorist-group/
12. Dylan Matthews, "20 years, $6 trillion, 900,000 lives", last modified September 11, 2021, *Vox*, accessed on November 6, 2021, at https://www.vox.com/22654167/cost-deaths-war-on-terror-afghanistan-iraq-911
13. "NATO and Afghanistan", last modified September 16, 2021, North Atlantic Treaty Organization, accessed on November 6, 2021, at https://www.nato.int/cps/en/natohq/topics_8189.htm
14. Connor Keane, *US Nation-Building in Afghanistan* (New York: 2016, Routledge–Taylor & Francis Group), p. 90.
15. Meridith McGraw, "Trump wanted out of Afghanistan. Now he wants to bomb it", last modified September 9, 2021, *Politico*, accessed on November 6, 2021, at https://www.politico.com/news/2021/09/09/trump-foreign-policy-doctrine-510780
16. "First target is to destroy Pakistan: ISIS-K blames Islamabad for Afghanistan chaos", last modified November 2, 2021, WION News, accessed on November 6, 2021, at https://www.wionews.com/south-asia/first-target-is-to-destroy-pakistan-isis-k-blames-islamabad-for-afghanistan-chaos-426088
17. Baktash Siawash, "Pakistan has a new divide-and-rule strategy for Taliban. It's called ISIS-K", last modified September 19, 2021, *The Print*, accessed on November 7, 2021, at ....
18. "Can Washington speed up special visa processing for Afghans", last modified July 2021, *The Diplomat*, accessed on November 7, 2021, at https://thediplomat.com/2021/07/can-washington-speed-up-special-visa-processing-for-afghans/
19. Keane, *US Nation-Building*, p. 2.
20. "Taliban bans foreign currencies in Afghanistan", last modified November 4, 2021, British Broadcasting Corporation (BBC), accessed on November 5, 2021, at https://www.bbc.com/news/business-59129470
21. "Meeting in Doha", last modified August 31, 2021, Ministry of External Affairs (MEA), Government of India, accessed on September 30, 2021, at https://mea.gov.in/press-releases.htm?dtl/34208/Meeting_in_Doha

7. Decoding Chinese Ambitions in Afghanistan: Its Implications on India

Suchita Sharma

PREVIEW
UNDERSTANDING AFGHANISTAN GEOPOLITICS

Brief History of the Region

Afghanistan, like many other states, was a victim of its history and geography. From peace to war, day to night, Afghanistan has faced all the seasons of wax and wane. The territorially bounded state formation of Afghanistan was rooted into contraction of colonialism. Initially, it was under tribal confederation and known as Kush Dynasty/Empire (until the 18th century). In the nineteenth century, Afghanistan emerged as a perfect buffer state between the British and Russian empires.[1] It is a known gateway between Asia and Europe. Britain annexed Afghanistan, which turned out as a series of Anglo-Afghan wars of 1838-1842, 1878-1880, 1919-1921).[2] In 1934, The United States formally recognised Afghanistan as an independent state. In the year 1937, a French diplomat René Dollot described Afghanistan as "Switzerland of Asia".[3] The tag indeed proved meaningful in history, because "Afghanistan was the most peaceful country in the Asian continent". Ironically, all this shifted into its second phase and this phrase again flipped on the other side of the coin.

In 1947, Britain withdrew from India. A whole new Islamic State of Pakistan emerged which ultimately became an immediate neighbour of Afghanistan. During this period, King Zahir Shah decided to introduce a so-called New liberal Democracy in Afghanistan. Concurrently, the US established defence relations with Pakistan in 1954 and Afghanistan leaned towards USSR's support. Soon, Daoud Khan gained power after staging a successful coup in Afghanistan. This was the era when Islamic (Sharia-dominant) organisations became the core and they had formed groups known as the *jihad fighters* or *mujahideen* (mostly based in Pakistan and Iran).[4] Thousands of Muslim radicals from Middle East, North Africa and other neighbouring countries also joined to support them. Amongst them was Osama bin Laden, who resided in Pakistan in the early 1980s and built several training facilities for foreign recruits inside Afghanistan. Massive support and funds were provided to him from secretive channels, basically to accomplish the mission of spreading terror.[5] In continuation of this, a group of Mujahideen commanders who called themselves as local warlords emerged and became known as the *Taliban*. Their stated objectives were to regain stability of the region and to follow *Sharia Islamic law* (their own interpretation of Islam). In 1995, the Taliban took control of city, Herat, their use of mobile warfare appeared as a strong indicator to change the regional atmosphere. Many innocent women and children faced huge suppression from the Taliban's ideology. In 1997, Osama bin Laden shook hands with the head of the Taliban, Mullah Muhammad Umar. Following the alliance of Islamic militias, they started showering harsh rules, narcotism, extortion, kidnapping, ransom and terror bombings in and around Afghanistan.

On September 11, 2001, they hijacked and crashed four commercial planes in the World Trade Center Towers at New York; the Pentagon outside Washington, DC and took a thousand lives in Pennsylvania field.[6] This event ultimately was recorded among the dark days of world history. In retaliation, the US and British forces launched air strikes against the Taliban and at all possible hideouts of Osama bin Laden. After a prolonged fight, the Taliban flew from Afghan territory to Pakistan. And declared "the rule of Taliban has totally ended". In 2003, amid the turmoil, NATO took hold of security in Kabul. The US and NATO forces pledged to maintain peace and stability, and their mission of "war on terror" began.[7]

Today (2021), after a 20-year intervention, Washington decided to discontinue its military presence in Afghanistan. A long dream of creating a western style national democracy and peace has failed miserably.[8] The US desires to make the world a better place by introducing undifferentiated rules and healthy democratic values turned into a nightmare for their long-stayed-home, Afghanistan. Following the exit of US forces, the Afghanistan government collapsed and the Taliban reinstated.

Geographical Explanation of Afghanistan

Afghanistan is a landlocked multi-ethnic country, situated in the heart of South-Central Asia. It is bounded to east and south by Pakistan (including the area of Indian [disputed] territory of Kashmir which is administered by Pakistan and known as Pakistan-Occupied Kashmir). To the west of Afghanistan lies Iran. Towards the north, Afghanistan touches the borders of Central Asian states—Tajikistan, Uzbekistan and Turkmenistan. It shares a border with China's Xinjiang province, at the north-eastern mountain ranges, which is known as Vakhān (Wakhan Corridor).[9]

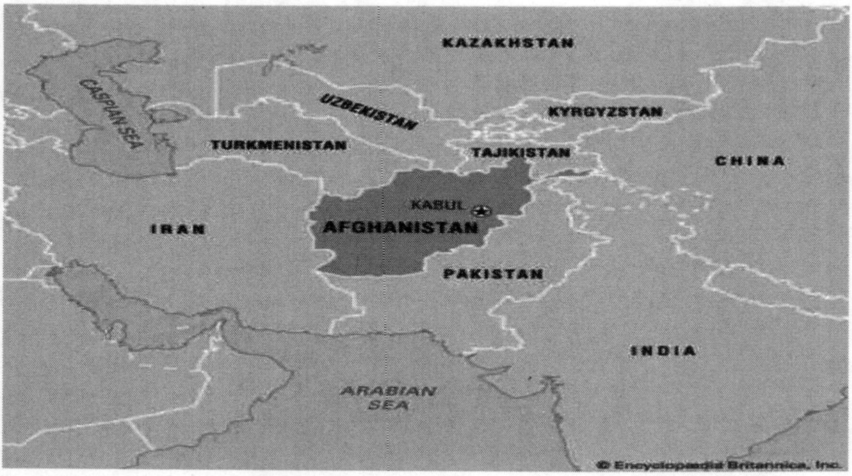

Source: Encyclopaedia Britannica. *Afghanistan*. Retrieved on October 6, 2021, from https://www.britannica.com/place/Afghanistan/Plant-and-animal-life_

Thus, the aim of this paper is divided into two parts. First, to analyse the main trend/pattern of involvement of China in Afghanistan. And secondly, the paper will attempt to considerably note the implications and concerns for India.

PART I
CHINA'S INVOLVEMENT IN AFGHANISTAN (POST- 9/11)

China has consistently maintained positive relations with its Afghan neighbours. After the United States invasion of Afghanistan in 2001, China was amongst the very first nations to institute their official relations with President Karzai, and had its embassy in Kabul in February 2002. At the end of the same year, both the nations inked the Declaration on "Good Neighbourly Relation".[10] The year 2005 witnessed Chinese association with Russia and Central Asian states through the Shanghai Cooperation Organisation–Afghanistan Contact Group to cope with Afghan instability.[11] China has also collaboratively worked on the Afghan peace process in several multilateral fronts, such as: China-Russia-Afghanistan, China-Pakistan-Afghanistan, China-Russia-US-Afghanistan, China-Iran-Afghanistan, and so on. In 2012, Beijing-Kabul signed five-pillar cooperation to strengthen their friendly relations—on Economy, Humanities, Politics, Security and International-Regional affairs. Therefore, it is pertinent to chart a new road to peace with the involvement of China, because of its track record and geographical proximity to Afghanistan.

China initially provided $ 5 million in emergency humanitarian aid, followed by a promise of providing reconstruction aid as well as diplomatic support as goodwill. Later, it ramped up its economic investment from billions to trillions. In 2014, President Ghani promoted talks with China for their involvement in regional connectivity and economic growth of the state.[12] The continuous indulgence resulted in the formation of the "Quadrilateral Coordination Group (QCG)" involving: Afghanistan, Pakistan, the USA and China, also known as New Quad. This group is believed to have a remarkable shift in world order. It will impart a single platform for American and Chinese political cooperation in the state of Afghanistan. China plays its cooperation card on the multiple issues, for example, security, trade, cultural and social integration.[13] It keeps active/visible military involvement away and tries to be on the good side of the card. Over the years, China's policy for Afghanistan has evolved from "calculated indifference to active engagement".[14]

On the economic front, China has always been a pro-ready foreign investor with the aim of being a Global player. In 2016, China and Afghanistan signed an MoU (Memorandum of Understanding) to promote collaboration in the BRI (Belt and Road Initiative). Launched in 2013, the Belt and Road project is an ambition of President Xi to expand infrastructure and connectivity. It is an everlasting policy aimed to connect Asia, Europe, and the African continent, vis-à-vis Road and Seas route. Hence, it is also known as OBOR—One Belt-One Road initiative. (Please refer to the following figure to have a better understanding of the BRI connectivity model for the continent.)

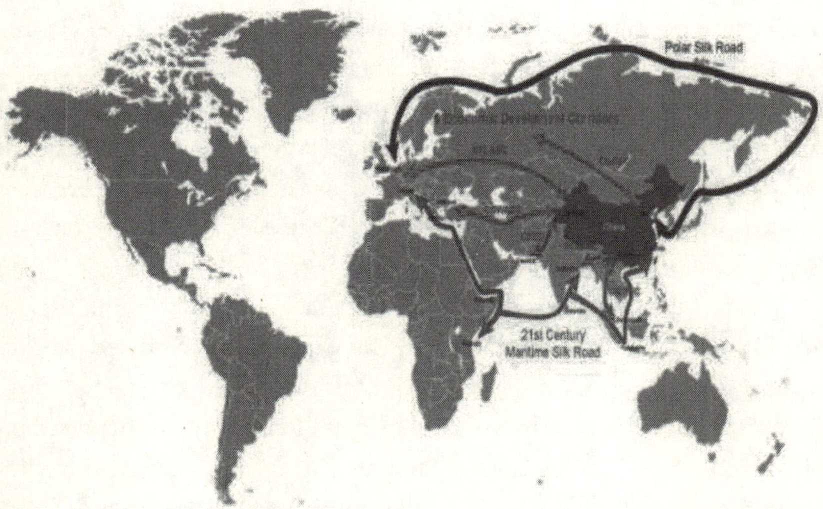

Source: *Belt and Road Initiative*. Retrieved on October 7, 2021, from https://www.beltroad-initiative.com/belt-and-road/

Subsequently, China provided a lucrative opportunity to Afghanistan to become a member of the Chinese-led Asian Infrastructure Investment Bank (AIIB).[15] Chinese aspiration is well proved in her active seizing of all the opportunities to show her economic strengths in almost all the South Asian nations (neighbours of India) and try to approach other low income/financially unstable countries. The trade connectivity was enhanced between the two countries in November 2018, when both inaugurated the Afghanistan-China Air corridor.

China has a strong strategic leverage over Pakistan, seen as an influential power with the potential of bringing some stability in the war-torn state. It has stepped forward to take part in a constructive role for improving Kabul-Islamabad relations.

Afghanistan is known for her untapped vast mineral reserves, which could be the future keyholder for the country's economy. A survey has been conducted by US Geologists and Pentagon that proves the deposits of Iron, Copper, Niobium and other minerals worth at least $ 1 trillion.[16] For Afghanistan, China largely invested in copper extraction, oil and gas sectors and railroad infrastructure. China had invested $ 3.5 billion in developing Aynak Copper Mines (located in the province of Logar), and thus established itself as Afghanistan's single largest foreign investor.[17] China has also planned to expand its resource exploration in Afghanistan. They intend to construct a new natural gas pipeline project named "TACT—Turkmenistan, Afghanistan, China, and Tajikistan".[18] As this has been labelled, it would serve the purpose of connecting Central Asia, China and Afghanistan. It would be logical to depict that, in coming years, TACT may connect other Gulf countries. Therefore, the post-US withdrawal economic policy of the Taliban will definitely cast China.

China is geographically linked to northern Afghanistan through Wakhan Corridor—a narrow strip of land extending towards China; touching Indian northern landmass (POK), separating Tajikistan and Pakistan by mountain ranges. These two countries agreed to set up a fibre-optic link passing through Wakhan corridor in the Badakhshan Province of Northern Afghanistan.[19] This will surely facilitate agricultural, mineral, and industrial connections between China and Afghanistan (may also be helpful for other next-door countries). In September 2018, an interview cited by *Reuters* revealed that China is ready to prepare/train Afghan soldiers, in order to counter ISIS and Al Qaeda militancy. Further, Intelligence agencies worldwide have circulated a report about the setting up of a Chinese military base in Wakhan Corridor which were the facilitators of building these training camps.[20, 21] Although China has frequently denied these reports,[22] it is certain, there is no smoke without fire. It would be early to comment on any of these. At the least, India or world intelligence needs to watch out for these kinds of smoke.

Geographically, it is pertinent to note that China and Pakistan are known to be "all-weather friends", the intimate strong relations of these two brother nations can be a significant factor to ensure a long-term stability of China in Afghanistan. Pakistan—once a country that hosted the Taliban—provided them financial and ideological support. Having said that, the China-Pak nexus can be seen as the China-Pak-Afghan nexus. This strategic manoevre would result in a diplomatic equilibrium of all sorts in this region.[23] This will reflect a dynamic change in regional geopolitics that can be a cause of concern for India on several fronts.

China's Security Concerns

This is unquestionable that China wants to enhance its diplomatic, economic and cultural engagement with Afghanistan. Although, Xi is watchful of Afghan being a latent breeding ground for Uyghur Muslims which may affect Xinjiang's peace in coming years. Afghanistan is home for a number of transnational terrorist organisations. Xinjiang is claimed as a region breeding evils, such as terrorism; religious extremism and separatism; and, thus, plaguing their own country.[24] Therefore, Uyghur-owned regions can be vulnerable for China. There can be some other notable concerns, first, Afghanistan is known for drug plantation and supply. It is a part of Golden Crescent comprising Iran, Afghanistan and Pakistan.

Secondly, China wants NATO withdrawal, as it can be a possible factor to impact on Beijing's transcontinental infrastructure project, which focuses on the chronic connectivity of China with Central Asia; North and East Africa; Southeast Asia and Gulf countries; and European states.[25] Third, and the most important factor, China needs to pay attention to its relationship with other regional powers; Afghanistan's stability won't be achieved by merely a single state assistance. It will need diplomatic interactions with other neighbours as well.

PART II
IMPLICATIONS AND CONCERNS FOR INDIA

India's stance in this present (2021) scenario is unavoidable. The future of Afghanistan looks unpredictable; bare and bleak. Now, India is left with very limited options for her points of concern. Following are some considerable projections and strategies to damp the risks.

Analysing Risk Factors

- **Terrorism.** The first and foremost major risk from war-torn Afghanistan is the possibility of international and regional terrorism. The security void created by the American withdrawal of their forces has resulted in the rise of IS-K (Islamic State-Khorasan), Haqqani networks and other self-proclaimed terror groups, that have started operating in South Asia and Central Asia. The Haqqani network which was believed to have anti-India agendas carried out attacks against Indian assets, namely, propaganda carried out in Kashmir and attack on Indian embassy in Kabul.[26] They can intensify their disruptive activities again in India and even in the South Asian region.
- **Pakistan's Influence.** The second calculated risk is the increasing influence of Pakistan in Afghanistan. As already mentioned in the chapter the Taliban had hideouts in Pakistan from/for a long time. It could be a matter of serious concern for India at the present moment, when the Taliban has full control over Afghanistan.[27]
- **China-Pak Nexus.** From past records, China was never a so friendly nation for India. Sino-Indian border disputes (on every front) stay hot in all seasons. Therefore, it is an unavoidable concern for India's security in future years. India's north-western territory, which touches the Wakhan corridor, is vulnerable under Pakistan's control. Thus, India needs to play tactically to keep Afghanistan away from the China-Pak Nexus.
- **Drug Trafficking.** Afghanistan, being a sole member of Golden Crescent, a huge distributor/supplier of drugs in and around South Asia, Central Asia, African and European nations. It would be imperative for India to keep a careful watch on these illegal and organised activities from the Talibani Emirate.

- **Refugee Crisis.** This kind of trouble in any state leads to people moving out in search of peaceful lands. Therefore, it can be considered a risk factor for the neighbouring countries of Afghanistan. For example, India, known for her welcoming and human nature. This time India needs to keep a careful watch on it, as it may sow seeds of terror/drug-human trafficking.

Analysing Mitigation Strategies for India

- Active Diplomatic Engagement
  1. To prevent Russia and Iran from joining the China-Pak-Taliban nexus. India needs to have strong diplomatic manoeuvres and back channel play.
  2. India needs to strengthen its hold on Chabahar and Jask ports to prevent ever-increasing influence of China into Iran.
  3. Expansion of QUAD can make a big difference. France, Britain, and Southeast Asian nations should come together to stop the emergence of China-Taliban-Pakistan.[28]
  4. India knew that the Chinese plan of BRI is to dominate and encircle Asia. It is a well-planned geo-economic strategy known as "String of Pearls" and "Silk Route" (sea and land, respectively). With this, China has created unsustainable debt drift for many Indian neighbours, which can be analysed as their *Debt-trap tactics* for low/developing or underdeveloped countries. For example, now it has targeted Afghanistan, where they have spent $ 3 billion on infra-projects.[29]
- Investment in Training and Development

  India needs to focus on long-term capacity building programmes, military training, developing intelligence networks. To lower the levels of violence, India should plan to indulge in peace talks/training/infra-development practices with the Taliban's government.[30]

Conclusion

"There is a cost to pay; for every strategy that comes into play".

For two decades, the US presence in Afghanistan was not appreciated and at the end it did not serve any predictable results of peace. In turn, it leaves Taliban hold over the land, making it more anxious and fragile. The Taliban's distinct ideology and perspective leave a tension for international entities. The present threat to Afghanistan needs to be recognised in a realist approach. Mere talks of talking with the Taliban is extremely unsettling for minor sections of the society.[31, 32] Sadly, global consent has failed to resolve or raise the unheard issues yielding on Afghanistan's ground.

What is however worrisome is witnessing China's foot in the state of Afghanistan. The goal of chinese economic and diplomatic engagement with the Taliban, will leave significant security challenges in the region. With visions of expanding their footprint in the form of Infrastructure Initiatives like BRI; OBOR; CPEC. Questions arise: Will China want to take over the US's role in Afghanistan? The answer to this could be a big NO. But, nevertheless, China wants to become a big player/global power for the continent. Thus, it won't miss this opportunity to occupy a stronghold in a Taliban-controlled country. On the other hand, China could be worried about ensuring that instability does not spread to Xinjiang province. The spread of extremism/militancy/insurgency is the mutual concern of China, India, Russia and Central Asian countries. Therefore, it is clear that China will secure its position with traditional, economic and diplomatic ways, but would not involve itself in any direct military means.

It will be too early to comment on India's stand in this mud. And, it can be too delayed to ignore the spillover effects of what's happening in our immediate neighbourhood (vis-à-vis China-Pak-Taliban intercourse). It cannot afford to be distant and has to develop its diplomatic ties with the Taliban, to make sure their economic, cultural, and developmental investments in Afghanistan will not go in vain. Hence, India should shore up her defences and keep an active watch on the changing geopolitics and geostrategy. Afghanistan is currently on a challenging plate, not only for India but for the whole world. Nevertheless, it would be better to assume that peace will prevail in Afghanistan; threatening clouds must clear the skies. The conclusion of this paper is based on the research and review of the current shifts in the region.

Notes

1. Maley, W. (2010). "Afghanistan: an historical and geographical appraisal", *International Review of the Red Cross* 92 (880), 1-18, at https://doi.org/10.1017/S1816383111000154
2. PBS NewsHour. (2011b, May 4). *A Historical Timeline of Afghanistan.* At https://www.pbs.org/newshour/politics/asia-jan-june11-timeline-afghanistan
3. René Dollot, *L'Afghanistan: Histoire, Description, Moeurs et Coutumes, Folklore, Fouilles* (Payot-Paris, 1937), p. 15.
4. Human Rights Watch, *Backgrounder on Afghanistan: History of the War*. Retrieved from https://www.hrw.org/legacy/backgrounder/asia/afghan-bck1023.pdf
5. Ibid.
6. PBS NewsHour, n. 2.
7. Ibid.
8. Michael, P. (2021, June 30). *What can we learn from the failed U.S. intervention in Afghanistan?, GIS Reports*. Geopolitical Intelligence Services. Retrieved from https://www.gisreportsonline.com/afghanistan-the-end-of-the-rules-based-world-order,3552,c.html
9. *Encyclopedia Britannica. Afghanistan*. Retrieved on October 6, 2021, from https://www.britannica.com/place/Afghanistan/Plant-and-animal-life
10. Joint Declaration between The People's Republic of China and The Islamic Republic of Afghanistan on Establishing Strategic and Cooperative Partnership, Ministry of Foreign Affairs of the People's Republic of China, at https://www.fmprc.gov.cn/mfa_eng/wjdt_665385/2649_665393/t939517.html
11. Chia, C., K. Kalachelvam and Z. Haiqi. (2021, June 25). *Exploring China's Afghanistan Policy*, at https://www.isas.nus.edu.sg/papers/exploring-chinas-afghanistan-policy/
12. Raghav Sharma, "Afghanistan: Discerning China's Westward March". *Asian Affairs*, 2009, at https://www.tandfonline.com/doi/abs/10.1080/03068374.2019.1672408?journalCode=raaf20
13. Ghosh, A. (2019, February 26). *China's growing influence in Afghanistan and its implications for the Peace Process*, at https://www.icwa.in/show_content.php?lang=1&level=3&ls_id=3856&lid=2935#_ftn12
14. Shubhangi Pandey, "Can China Drive the Afghan Peace Process?", *The Diplomat*, May 18, 2019.
15. Chia, n. 11.
16. James Risen, "U.S. Identifies Vast Mineral Riches in Afghanistan", *New York Times*, June 13, 2010; Alissa J. Rubin, "Afghan Officials Elated by Minerals Report", *New York Times*.
17. Michael Wines, "China Willing to Spend Big on Afghan Commerce", *New York Times*, December 30, 2009.
18. A. Peterson, "Afghanistan Has What China Wants", *Foreign Policy*, at https://foreignpolicy.com/2013/04/18/afghanistan-has-what-china-wants/

19. Shubhangi Pandey, "Understanding China's Afghanistan Policy: From Calculated Indifference to Strategic Engagement", Issue Brief No. 305, August 2019, Observer Research Foundation.
20. "China says it is helping Afghanistan with defense, counterterrorism", Reuters, at https://www.reuters.com/article/us-china-afghanistan/china-says-it-is-helping-afghanistanwith-defense-counterterrorism-idUSKCN1LF13H
21. Saraswat, A. (2020, April 17). "Chinese Interests in Afghanistan: From Indifference to Strategic Involvement". *Diplomatist*. https://diplomatist.com/2020/04/17/chinese-interests-in-afghanistan-from-indifference-to-strategic-involvement/
22. "China denies having troops in Afghanistan's Wakhan Corridor", *Military Times*, February 28, 2018, at https://www.militarytimes.com/flashpoints/2019/03/01/china-denies-having-troops-inafghanistans-wakhan-corridor/
23. Farhan Bokhari, "China has economic aims as it quietly builds bonds with Afghanistan", *Nikkei Asian Review*, at https://asia.nikkei.com/Spotlight/Belt-and-Road/China-has-economicaims-as-it-quietly-builds-bonds-with-Afghanistan
24. Andrew Small, "China's Caution on Afghanistan-Pakistan", *The Washington Quarterly*, pp. 81-82, at https://csis-prod.s3.amazonaws.com/s3fs-public/legacy_files/files/publication/twq10julysmall.pdf
25. Shubhangi Pandey, n. 19.
26. Sirajuddin Haqqani. (February 20, 2020). "What We, the Taliban, Want", *New York Times*, https://www.nytimes.com/2020/02/20/opinion/taliban-afghanistan-war-haqqani.html
27. Chaudhuri, R., and S. Shende. (2020). "Dealing With the Taliban: India's Strategy in Afghanistan after U.S. Withdrawal", Carnegie India, pp. 11-13, at https://carnegieendowment.org/files/Chaudhuri_Shende_-_Afghanistan.pdf
28. Garg, V. (2021, August 3). "Scenario in Afghanistan and Options with Compulsions for India", Commodore Vijesh Kumar Garg, VSM | C3S India | Chennai Centre for China Studies, at https://www.c3sindia.org/defence-security/scenario-in-afghanistan-and-options-with-compulsions-for-india-commodore-vijesh-kumar-garg-vsm/
29. Chatzky, A., and J. McBribe. (2020, January 28). "China's Massive Belt and Road Initiative", Council on Foreign Relations, at https://www.cfr.org/backgrounder/chinas-massive-belt-and-road-initiative
30. Chaudhuri and Shende, n. 27.
31. Maley, W. (2010). "Afghanistan: an historical and geographical appraisal", *International Review of the Red Cross 92*, (880), 1-18. https://doi.org/10.1017/S1816383111000154
32. "The 'Ten Dollar' Talib and Women's Rights", *Human Rights Watch*, New York, 2010.

References

A. Peterson. "Afghanistan Has What China Wants". *Foreign Policy*. Available at: https://foreignpolicy.com/2013/04/18/afghanistan-has-what-china-wants/

Abdul Qadir Sediqi and Rupam Jain. "Afghanistan's Taliban meets the Chinese government in Beijing". Reuters. Available at https://www.reuters.com/article/us-afghanistan-taliban-china/afghanistans-taliban-meets-chinese-government-in-beijing-idUSKBN1W70I3

Chatzky, A., and J. McBribe. (2020, January 28). "China's Massive Belt and Road Initiative". Council On Foreign Relations. Available at: https://www.cfr.org/backgrounder/chinas-massive-belt-and-road-initiative

Chaudhuri, R., and S. Shende. (2020). "Dealing with the Taliban: India's Strategy in Afghanistan after U.S. Withdrawal". Available at: https://carnegieendowment.org/files/Chaudhuri_Shende_-_Afghanistan.pdf

E.W. Jolly. "China Considers Larger Role in Afghan Peace Process". *The New York Times*. Available at: http://www.nytimes.com/2016/01/25/world/asia/china-considers-larger-role-in-afghanistan-peace-process.html?_r=0

Garg, V. (2021, August 3). "Scenario in Afghanistan and Options with Compulsions for India". Commodore Vijesh Kumar Garg, VSM | C3S India | Chennai Centre for China Studies. Available at: https://www.c3sindia.org/defence-security/scenario-in-afghanistan-and-options-with-compulsions-for-india-commodore-vijesh-kumar-garg-vsm/

Ghosh, A. (2019, February 26). "China's growing influence in Afghanistan and its implications for the Peace Process". Available at: https://www.icwa.in/show_content.php?lang=1&level=3&ls_id=3856&lid=2935#_ftn12

Ghulam Ali. "China-Pakistan Cooperation on Afghanistan: Assessing Key Interests and Implementing Strategies". *The Pacific Review* (2020).

Grossman, D. (2021, January 22). "China and the Taliban Begin Their Romance". Available at: https://www.rand.org/blog/2021/07/china-and-the-taliban-begin-their-romance.html

Grossman, D. *What China Wants In South Asia | ORF*. Available at: https://www.orfonline.org/research/what-china-wants-in-south-asia-67665/

https://www.gisreportsonline.com/afghanistan-the-end-of-the-rules-based-world-order,3552,c.html

Maley, W. (2010). "Afghanistan: an historical and geographical appraisal". *International Review of the Red Cross* 92, (880), 1-18. Available at: https://doi.org/10.1017/S1816383111000154

Maninder Dabas. "Here is All You Should Know About 'String of Pearls', China's Strategy to Encircle India", *India Times*. Available at: https://www.indiatimes.com/news/india/here-is-all-you-should-know-about-string-of-pearls-china-s-policy-to-encircle-india-324315.html

Michael Martina. "China Will Not Fill U.S. Void in Afghanistan: Official". Reuters. Available at: http://www.reuters.com/article/2014/07/21/us-china-afghanistanid USKBN0FQ12I20140721

Michael Wines, "China Willing to Spend Big on Afghan Commerce". *New York Times*, December 30, 2019.

Michael, P. (2021, June 30). "What can we learn from the failed U.S. intervention in Afghanistan?". GIS Reports P. Geopolitical Intelligence Services.

NewsHour, P. (2011, May 4). "A Historical Timeline of Afghanistan". PBS NewsHour. Available at: https://www.pbs.org/newshour/politics/asia-jan-june11-timeline-afghanistan

Petersen, A. "Afghanistan Has What China Wants". *Foreign Policy*. Retrieved on October 10, 2021. Available at: https://foreignpolicy.com/2013/04/18/afghanistan-has-what-china-wants/

Raghav Sharma. "Afghanistan: Discerning China's Westward March". *Asian Affairs*, 2009. Available at: https://www.tandfonline.com/doi/abs/10.1080/03068374.2019.1672408?journalCode=raaf20

Shakti Sinha, "Talking to the Taliban: 'India Must Ride the Tide at Its Flood'". *StratNews Global*. Available at: https://stratnewsglobal.com/talking-to-the-taliban-india-must-ride-the-tide-at-its-flood/

Sirajuddin Haqqani. "What We, the Taliban, Want". *New York Times*. Available at: https://www.nytimes.com/2020/02/20/opinion/taliban-afghanistan-war-haqqani.html

Suhasini Haidar. "We Will Build Ties in the Neighbourhood: Taliban". *The Hindu*, April 24, 2020. Available at: https://www.thehindu.com/news/international/we-will-build-ties-in-the-neighbourhood-taliban/

Suhasini Haider and Dinakar Peri. "China Accuses India of Trespass, Line of Actual Control Heats Up". *The Hindu*. Available at: https://www.thehindu.com/news/national/tensions-escalate-along-lac-in-sikkim-as-china-accuses-india-of-trespass/article31629997.ece

Sumedha Korishetti. "Challenges to state control of territory: Comparative analysis of Yemen, Afghanistan and Myanmar". *Asian Journal of Comparative Politics*, 2021.

Tom Hussain. "What China Has to Fear from a U.S.-Taliban Peace Deal in Afghanistan". *South China Morning Post*. Available at: https://www.scmp.com/week-asia/politics/article/3051861/what-china-has-fear-ustaliban-peace-deal-afghanistan.

Zhao Huasheng. "China and Afghanistan: China's interest, stances and perspective". Centre for Strategic and International Studies, p. 2. Available at: https://csis-prod.s3.amazonaws.com/s3fs-public/legacy_files/files/publication/120322_Zhao_ChinaAfghan_web.pdf

"India Readying Rapid Response Teams for Bangladesh, Bhutan, Sri Lanka and Afghanistan". *The Hindu*. Available at: https://www.thehindu.com/news/national/coronavirus-india-readying-teams-forbangladesh-bhutan-sri-lanka-afghanistan/article31398453.ece

"India to Use Chabahar Port to Send Assistance to Afghanistan". *The Hindu*. Available at: https://www.thehindu.com/news/national/india-to-use-chabahar-port-to-send-assistance-toafghanistan/article31326064.ece

"Taliban in China to Discuss Afghan Peace After US Talks Collapse". *Al Jazeera*. Available at: https://www.aljazeera.com/news/2019/09/taliban-china-discuss-afghan-peace-talkscollapse-190923090323341.html

8. Regional Security Complex in South Asia: A Study of the Rise of Taliban in Afghanistan

Puyesh Kant Sharma

Introduction

"Security" is often defined as the lack of vulnerabilities and dangers to certain values that can bring in the feeling of being safe. Security issues present a serious risk to a designated "referent object"[1] and rationalise the use of different measures to handle them.[2] It specifies the circumstances by which protection can be achieved. Its logical clarification paves the way to explore the required conditions of security and recognition of such situations that provides foundation for the growth of this concept.[3] Barry Buzan in his book *Security: A New Framework for Analysis* laid the theoretical foundation of regional security complex.[4] It also leads to the broadening, deepening and extending of security studies in post-Cold War era.

The traditional security study defines the field limited to military and territorial integrity of the state.[5] It argues that any attempt to widen the concept of security beyond military security would confuse intellectual coherence of the subject. "If all the forces that threaten life, property and wellbeing are considered as threat to our national security, then the meaning of security will become vague and all large scale evils will become threat to national security."[6] Military security is considered as the referent object and any other issue of security is essential only if it enhances the military security of the state.[7] Jef Huysmans argues that enhancing the security agenda from traditional to non-traditional spheres like societal, environmental, economic, identity, resources and so on has opened intense discussion of security agenda as it has neglected the meaning and significance of security itself.[8] But with the disintegration of the USSR and resultant shrinkage of bipolar challenge between the US and USSR, expansion of globalisation, growth of institutions like World Bank and World Trade Organizations, there was a surge of identity-related conflicts and regional security challenges.

Regional Security Complex Theory (RSCT) brings forth the dynamics of the political and military concerns because challenges in these sectors travel more easily over short distances than over long ones, so distance clearly plays a role in producing regional security complexes. RSCT helps to understand the emergence of new structures in post-Cold War era. It evaluates the relative balance of power and mutual relationship between regional and global dynamics. RSCT distinguishes between the interplay of the global and regional powers where less powerful countries whose main security environment is their local region becomes more pertinent. The central idea in RSCT is that the threats travel more easily over short distances than over long ones, therefore the security interdependence is normally patterned into regionally based clusters.

Friedberg argues that "the most states historically have been concerned primarily with the capabilities and intentions of their neighbours. Processes of securitisation and the degree of security interdependence are more intense between the actors inside such complexes than they are between actors inside the complex and those outside it."[9] RSCT offers a conceptual framework that classifies security regions into a set of types and provides a basis for comparative studies in regional security. It also offers a theory with some powers of prediction, in the sense of being able to narrow the range of possible outcomes for given types of region.[10]

The radical extremist organisations and violent religious movements in South Asia bring serious concerns to the practices of security and integrity of States in the region. Because such organisations and movements threaten the ideas of liberty, equality, justice, secularism and democratic polity of nation states. It also threatens the interreligious harmony, social fabric, security and territorial integrity of States in South Asia. As such, religious extremism, terrorism, drug trafficking and arms smuggling are viewed by various countries in South Asia as the main threats to their security and integrity.

The extremist ideologies and practices like that of Wahhabi and Taliban groups are intolerant of other cultures and religions. These fundamentalist movements in Asia in general and South Asia in particular are the main source of instability and conflict in this region. The emergence of such movements has been influenced by the leading ideologues of Islamic fundamentalist thought including that of "Sheikh Muhammad ibn-Abd-al-Wahab, Jamal-ud-Din Afghani, Ali Shariati, Ayatollah Ruhullah Khomeini, the leader of the Islamic Republic of Iran, Hassan-al-Banna founder of the Ikhwan-al-Muslameen (Muslim Brotherhood) and Sayyid Qutb of the Muslim Brotherhood of Egypt and Maulana Syed Abul Ala Mawdudi of Pakistan—the first Amir of the Jamaat-e-Islami."[11] These ideologues emphasised that political power is indispensable to the establishment of an Islamic state.

The emphasis by the Islamist radicals on the supremacy of their ideology and practice of pan-Islamism which is based on the concept of Ummah (community of believers), transcending national boundaries, ethnicities, creeds, race and all other distinctions is at the root of violence, conflict and instability in parts of South Asia. Talibanism as an ideology is an ardent attempt to imbibe the medieval times Islamic principles in different parts of the world in general and Islamic world in particular. The return of Taliban to power in Afghanistan is a matter of triumph for these fundamentalists and means to idealise the return of Islamic Caliphate wherever possible. It has brought forth the dynamics of the political and military concerns and put forth considerable challenge to social and identity security in the region. This has threatened the democratic values, secular character, pluralistic social order and communal harmony.[12] The paradigm shift in Afghanistan has complicated the regional security complex in South Asia.

Security Complex in South Asia

The end of the Cold War has changed the world from a bipolar to unipolar world, from closed economy to open economy and from traditional security to non-traditional security concerns. The New Cold War that began after Union of Soviet Socialist Republics (USSR) annexed Afghanistan became the hotbed of a war which had become dormant after the end of the Cold War and disintegration of the USSR. However, the United States of America (USA) returned to Afghanistan in 2001 on the pretext of "War on Terror" after the 9/11 Terror incident on World Trade Centre in New York. This has established a new security complex in South Asia with two nuclear power countries—India and Pakistan—at the centre of the region and Afghanistan at the core of world politics. India drifted more towards the USA, and Pakistan towards China, which again created a "security dilemma"[13] in the region. Politically, India supported the Hamid Karzai regime alongside the USA and Pakistan supported the return of the Taliban in Afghanistan.

The post-Cold War era has witnessed Af-Pak region as the epicentre of global terrorism and fought against it. The anti-terror war in Afghanistan that began in 2001 still continues. The sudden return of the Taliban to power in Afghanistan in August 2021 left the US-led North Atlantic Treaty Organization (NATO) forces with an unpleasant surprise. There is hardly any doubt that the country is likely to remain unstable for the foreseeable future and will remain a global hotspot for terrorist related issues. In the meantime, the war has a profound impact on regional and international security. In particular, it appears to have complicated South Asia's security relationships which added another dimension to the region's historical pattern of conflict.[14]

In Bangladesh, the rise of Islamic extremism brings security challenges that includes interregional and intraregional security. The fundamentalist organisations in Bangladesh, by aligning with the anti-India insurgents and terror outfits in India, challenge India's unity and territorial integrity. Radical Islam propagated in Bangladesh questions the normative foundations of democracy in the region. The aim of all the terrorist organisations in the region is essentially the same—the creation of a Shariah-governed region and establishment of Islamic Caliphate for the whole world. Bangladesh, with radical Islam as its political ideology, anti-India activities and sentiments, anti-secularism and anti-democracy well connected to international terror outfits, is a safe haven for Islamist terrorism.[15]

It is the new hotbed of international Islamist terrorism. Bangladesh is a major transit point for terrorist organisations in the whole of South Asia and even beyond. As a result, Bangladesh has emerged as a security concern to the whole of South Asia. Further, the resurgence of the Taliban in Afghanistan, deepening Islamisation of polity and society in Pakistan and beyond, slow but steady radicalisation taking place in the Maldives and Kashmir, rapidly rising local jihadi cells in India and the Islamisation of Bangladesh have tremendous potential to complicate the security scenario in entire South Asia.[16]

Here it becomes essential to analyse the role of South Asian Association for Regional Cooperation (SAARC) to maintain the security apparatus of the region. SAARC has been in existence for about three decades but its contribution and achievements towards conflict resolution and management is comparatively low. SAARC followed the European model, adopted the functional approach to build SAARC and amass similar benefits from regional understanding and cooperation. It was also expected to make significant impact to reduce political and military tensions among regional states, particularly between the two nuclear power states—India and Pakistan. But SAARC could neither achieve these goals nor is it able to overcome the trust deficit among nation states.[17]

At the end of the Cold War in 1990, many thought that SAARC would be able to live up to its full potential in a new international order. It was predicted that the developing regions would reap benefits from the end of the Cold War in terms of political, economic and security upliftment. Analysts suggested that in the unipolar world regional efforts would be beneficial and would bring economic prosperity for the region. However, in the case of South Asia, South Asian Free Trade Agreement (SAFTA) Framework which was designed to accelerate trade, investment and production across South Asia by removing all kinds of tariff and non-tariff barriers could not bring necessary dynamism for regional cooperation. Analysts have stated that the absence of politico-security confidence building mechanism among SAARC members is the key reason why the organisation has not functioned properly. The deliberate exclusion of the issues of high politics such as border disputes, inter-State terrorism and ethno-nationalism, etc., and Indo-Pak rivalry at SAARC meetings has not helped the organisation. These concerns have systematically raised the security issues in the region.

Revival of Taliban and Its Impact on South Asia

Following a coup d'état by Afghan communists in April 1978 and a Soviet invasion to bolster the cause of socialist revolution in December 1979, the mujahedin had managed to resist and eventually repel the Red Army. In 1979, Soviet aggression led to the overthrow of the People's Democratic Party of Afghanistan (PDPA) followed by the invasion of Afghanistan by the USSR. In combination with the Soviet intervention, the PDPA's socialist policies appeared to the people of Afghanistan as a challenge to their cultural and Islamic values. This misunderstanding was used by the ultra-conservative groups and ignited the religious fear psychosis to create local resistance groups who carried out jihad and called themselves as mujahedin. At that time, the United States supported these violent groups against its Cold War arch rival the USSR backed government in Kabul. Afghanistan became an active battleground between the two Superpowers. The US also formed diplomatic alliances with other Islamic countries, chiefly Saudi Arabia, Egypt, and Pakistan to counter Afghan mujahedin.

This effort was significantly expanded during the Reagan administration and carried forward by the active involvement of US Central Intelligence Services. In the meanwhile Saudi Arabia provided financial assistance to the US, Egypt became the main military supplier and training ground, while Pakistan offered military and civilian assistance to the Afghan resistance fighters and refugees and engaged in training and recruitment. Pakistan's president general, Muhammad Zia-ul-Haq, awarded his Inter-Services Intelligence (ISI) agency a monopoly over the distribution, training and shipment of military and financial assistance to the Afghan resistance groups.

Between 1994 and 1996, the Taliban achieved a succession of remarkable strategic victories against their mujahedin rivals. In September

1995 they captured the western town of Herat, and in September 1996 they took the eastern town of Jalalabad. Within only two years, they had gained control of most of the country. They organised air, armour, and infantry assaults in some locales. They negotiated their way into others, becoming the masters of many towns and villages without firing a shot. They gained the support of the Pashtuns, the group commonly identified as the largest ethnic group in Afghanistan and won the patronage of Pakistan, Saudi Arabia and the United Arab Emirates. In September 1996 the Taliban captured Kabul. While their leaders sought recognition as the winners of the Afghan civil war, the Taliban simultaneously launched a theatrical and bloody campaign to impose their vision of Islamic discipline on Kabul's residents. This is how this extremist group was made a terrorist group later, particularly in post 9/11 era.[18]

However, the Taliban rebels officially ended their regime way back in December 2001 and brought a halt to Afghanistan's Taliban Islamic Movement. Its leaders fled Kabul and had lost control over Afghanistan. Taliban leader Mullah Muhammad Omar Mujahed renounced his remaining political power and lost its control over Kandahar, the place where the Taliban originated. This led to the fall of the Taliban regime in 2001.[19] The attack on World Trade Centre in New York prompted the US to launch a military campaign against the Taliban regime and declared "War on Terror" against the Al Qaeda terrorist network. The campaign against Al Qaeda was named "Operation Enduring Freedom" and launched aerial bombardments and missile attacks. This signalled the beginning of the end of the Taliban regime's rule over Afghanistan.[20]

Though the Taliban was dormant after it was ousted it was never uprooted from Afghanistan and they started uniting and emerging again. By the time US President Barack Obama came to office in January 2009, the revival of the Taliban was evident. The Taliban re-emerged and expanded its territorial control in the Pashtun dominated areas. It carried out ferocious attacks on US bases across Afghanistan which started as early as 2007.[21] It became even more evident after NATO troops started leaving Afghanistan from 2012. The Taliban are resurgent not only in Afghanistan but also in Pakistan where the militants are engaged in armed conflict for control of the country's Federally Administered Northwest Tribal Areas.[22]

Here it is pertinent to analyse the role of the media on the one side and the political economy of Taliban's resurgence in Afghanistan on the other. There has been a rise in the Taliban's mobile phone text messages that encouraged the rural population to cooperate with them and defy the central government. The Taliban official online magazine, *Al Somood* has successfully propagated its ideas and intentions which has significant impact on the masses. Besides, Al Emarah, the official Taliban website, offers material in five different languages—Dari, Pashtu, Urdu, Arabic and English by the Taliban media cell.

In terms of its political economy, from 2005 to 2010, the Taliban's share of opium production and trafficking is put at between $ 90 million and $ 160 million a year, according to the UN Office on Drugs and Crime. In an alarming trend, opium poppy cultivation rose substantially in 2012, meaning higher profits and consequently a more vibrant insurgency. Higher production was driven by high prices for the crop, as well as by increased instability in the growing areas, making it easier for illicit networks to operate more freely. The money, thus generated, was enough to run an effective insurgency in the country. According to Russian officials, "by late 2013 almost 1,900 organized criminal groups and 150 major drug cartels in Central Asia were trafficking illicit drugs from Afghanistan to Russia" which was just the tip of the iceberg.[23]

Taliban in Afghanistan and Regional Security Complex of South Asia

As far as South Asian region is concerned, the majority of States in South Asia shared almost similar historical growth. They have emerged as Sovereign Nation States at the end of British colonial rule in the region in the middle of the twentieth century. In many ways, the history of the creation of these states holds the key to understanding some of the current hostilities within and among them.[24] The presence of Taliban regime in the 1990s coincides with armed conflicts in various parts of South Asia that includes militancy in Jammu and Kashmir, Naga Insurgent Movement in North East India,

Naxalite Movement in Middle India, Ethnic Conflict in Bangladesh, civil war in Nepal and LTTE sponsored violence in Sri Lanka.

There is historical evidence that the Afghanistan is a doorway to South Asia and any political, economic and military change in Afghanistan has direct impact on South Asian region. The withdrawal of US Security forces in haste in August 2021 from Afghanistan resulted in the Pakistan-backed Taliban forces capturing power in Kabul. This has created an enormously perilous situation in South Asia countries which can lead to the re-emergence of armed rebellion in various parts of South Asian countries.

Pakistan supported the Taliban in the 1990s but the American invasion in 2001 changed Pakistan's policy upside down and it joined US forces against the Taliban and Al Qaeda. Pakistan has been at the forefront of hosting Afghan refugees as well as offering aid and assistance towards US reconstruction efforts. However, Pakistan continued to support the Taliban, which became evident in recent times.

India, on the other hand, enjoyed better relations with Afghan governments except during the years of Taliban rule. After the fall of Taliban regime in 2001, India has actively invested in the reconstruction and development of Afghanistan, by contributing US$ 3 billion in developmental assistance. The most significant infrastructure development included the Salma Dam in Herat, the Zaranj-Delaram highway on the border with Iran and the Afghan Parliament house in Kabul. The sudden withdrawal of the US presented the South Asian region in general and India in particular a challenging regional landscape which can enhance India-Pakistan tensions along with India-China hostility. Many political pundits have predicted that the anti-state actors can make ardent attempts to revive themselves in India considering the presence of anti-India attitude of three of its neighbours, i.e., Pakistan, China and now Afghanistan. In this state of affairs RSCT, as put forward by Barry Buzan, can be contextualised in the case of South Asian region.

RSCT is largely based on the premise that region is basically a connected whole in terms of its socio-economic, politico-military and cultural dynamics, and any changes or challenges in one part can travel faster and have greater impact in the region. The revival of the Taliban in Afghanistan poses serious security dilemma for the South Asian states. Here the role of the interregional actors, particularly China, the US and Russia, becomes pertinent as their interference is a regional security threat. China and Pakistan have supported the new Taliban regime on the one side, and on the other India and the US have unsuccessfully tried to establish democratic regime in Afghanistan in the last two decades. This balance of power game in South Asian region and actions of global players has created regional security complex which was theorised by Barry Buzan in his book, *Security: A New Framework for Analysis.*

Conclusion

Afghanistan, also called the "Graveyard of Empires", is notoriously a difficult country to govern and can be called the heartland of Asia because of its geostrategic location. This landlocked country is a corridor for connecting South Asia, Central Asia, West Asia and the Indian Ocean. That is why historically the dominant powers of the world have unsuccessfully tried to control and govern this land. The floodgates of Indian subcontinent open through this country, therefore, all the great empires of history and powers have militarily and economically invested in Afghanistan. The US, after the 9/11 incident, tried to control and govern Afghanistan which proved futile within a decade, and was evident after NATO forces started pulling out from Afghanistan. However, the sudden withdrawal in mid-August 2021 has left the world in shock, and South Asia in the lurch.

When the Taliban came to power in the 1990s, South Asian region became more volatile which enhanced militancy in Jammu and Kashmir, Naga Insurgent Movement in North East India, Naxalite Movement in Middle India, Ethnic Conflict in Bangladesh, civil war in Nepal and LTTE sponsored violence in Sri Lanka. The coming of the Taliban to control the State and government of Afghanistan can be a call of revivalism of all anti-state actors and organisations in South Asia, particularly the terrorist groups who seek allegiance to Al Qaeda, Islamic State and terrorism.

In this state of affairs, the Taliban in Afghanistan poses vulnerabilities and risk to the South Asian regional security complex having "terrorism and armed rebellion" as a referent object of security. In volatile South Asia, which is already brimming with many other regional, ethnic, identity and inter-border conflicts, the Taliban in Afghanistan poses serious challenges for regional security. Since its independence in 1947, India has been dealing with threats from almost all its international borders including Pakistan, Afghanistan, China, Bangladesh, Sri Lanka and Nepal. However, the Taliban in Afghanistan, which is historically anti-India and pro-Pakistan, is a clear threat to the internal and external security of India. Moreover, the failure of the SAARC organisation to work cooperatively and consensually is in reality a regional security issue. The Taliban will always use its religious rhetoric by using and interpreting the religious texts in a way which suits them, and hence to justify whatever they do; however, the most pertinent way out for South Asian States is to act collectively and in cooperation through SAARC which is essential to prioritise the regional security of South Asia as a whole.

Notes

1. Security is always tied to a particular referent object to internal/external locations that needs to be secured including state, individual, ethnic group, environment or the planet itself. Cited in Barry Buzan and Lene Hansen, *The Evolution of International Security Studies* (New York: Cambridge University Press, 2009), pp. 10-11.
2. Ibid.
3. David Baldwin, "The Concept of Security", *Review of International Studies*, vol. 23, no. 1, 1997, p. 7.
4. Barry Buzan et al., *Security: A New Framework for Analysis* (Boulder, CO: Lynne Rienner Publishers, 1998).
5. Beatrice de Graaf and Cornel Zwierlein, "Historicizing Security—Entering the Conspiracy Dispositive", *Historical Social Research*, Leibniz Institute for Social Sciences, vol. 38, no. 1, 2013, p. 47.
6. Daniel Deudney, "The Case against Linking Environmental Degradation and Security", *Millennium Journal of International Studies*, vol. 19, no. 3, 1990, p. 461.
7. Lawrence Freedman, "International Security: Changing Targets", *Foreign Policy*, no. 110, 1998, pp. 52-53.
8. Jef Huysmans, "Security! What do you mean? From Concept to Thick Signifier", *European Journal of International Relations*, vol. 4, no. 2, 1998, p. 226.
9. Aaron L. Friedberg, "Ripe for Rivalry: Prospects for Peace in a Multipolar Asia", *International Security*, vol. 18, no. 3, 1993-1994, p. 5.

10. Ibid.
11. K. Warikoo (ed.), *Religion and Security in South and Central Asia* (London: Routledge, 2011), p. 1.
12. Ibid., p. 78.
13. Security Dilemma, though a key concept in IR theory, is most understudied empirically. The term is generally used to denote the self-defeating aspect of the quest for security in an anarchic system. According to this theory, even when no state has any desire to attack others, none can be sure that others' intentions are peaceful, or will remain so; hence, each must accumulate power for defence. Since no state can know that the power accumulation of others is defensively motivated only, each must assume that it might be intended for attack. Consequently, each party's power increments are matched by the others, and all wind up with no more security than when the vicious cycle began, along with the costs incurred in having acquired and having to maintain their power. Cited in Glenn H. Snyder, "The Security Dilemma in Alliance Politics", *World Politics,* Cambridge University Press, vol. 36, no. 4, July 1984, p. 461.
14. Bhimitra Chakma (ed.), *South Asia in Transition: Democracy, Political Economy and Security* (UK: Palgrave Macmillan, 2014), p. 3.
15. K. Warikoo (ed.), *Religion and Security in South and Central Asia* (London: Routledge, 2011), p. 122.
16. Ibid., p. 123.
17. Bhimitra Chakma (ed.), *South Asia in Transition: Democracy, Political Economy and Security* (UK: Palgrave Macmillan, 2014), p. 238.
18. Robert D. Crews and Amin Tarzai (eds.), *The Taliban and Crisis of Afghanistan* (London: Harvard University Press, 2008), p. 5.
19. Ibid., p. 274.
20. Ibid., p. 277.
21. Hassan Abbas, *The Taliban Revival: Violence and Extremism on Pakistan Afghanistan Frontier* (London: Yale University Press, 2014), p. 168.
22. Ibid., p. 1.
23. Ibid., pp. 175, 181.
24. Monika Bharthwal Datta, *Understanding Security Practices in South Asia* (New York: Routledge, 2012), p. 2.

9. Convulsed Women's Rights in Afghanistan Pursuant to Taliban Governance in Early Twenty-first Century

Rekha Kumari R. Singh

Introduction

Positive growth of Human Civilisation demands attainment of equality amongst human beings, amongst others, gender equality is the most essential aspect that needs a heed. Gender equality can aid elimination of all forms of discrimination against men, women and other genders. The vulnerability of women has been noticed since ancient times across the globe. The United Nations in its various reports has observed that women around the world suffer abuse of their rights, affecting their lives at large, and it's very important to protect the rights of this pregnable group.

The United Nations must address women's rights across countries to secure their progress and from time to time intervene, considering constant changes in women's practical lives with novel manifestation of discriminations which emerge over time. Discrimination against women varies from nation to nation based on their nationality, religion, education, disability, socio-economic status, etc.

One of the instances which can be observed with the recent takeover of Afghanistan by the Taliban is the position of women's rights. It has curtailed the freedom of girls and women with restrictions in respect of their movability, pursuance of education, being alone away from homes.

Such restrictions on women and girls are violations of their basic human rights that result in discrimination against the gender of highest order, which affects them in all respects—mentally, emotionally, physically, socially and economically—and need to be avoided at all costs.

Women's Rights in Afghanistan

The status of women in Afghanistan has remained subject to a number of conflicts since time immemorial, in which the efforts to improve their position and fulfilling their basic needs was constantly on the agenda. King Amanullah Khan who pushed for westernisation introduced the new constitution inspired by Mustafa Kemal Ataturk which guarantees rights of women equal to men. A number of evil practices such as child marriage, women no longer to be permitted to wear veil, polygamy, etc., were minimised. It emphasised opportunity of participation in right to vote during 1964, and also allowed them to be elected to office, can get jobs, can also run businesses and enter politics, which was due to the efforts made in the new constitution by Zahir Shah, who ruled as the last king of Afghanistan. But the traditional approach always rooted to protest on the entitlements of rights to women. In the beginning of growth of women, such a mentality could result in eroding their development due to civil war. In 1989, the Taliban formed their movement among the youth and gained popularity wherein they promised peace but, in reality, they were oppressive towards women wherein they curtailed rights of women to go to school, to the work place, forced to bear burqa which required to cover entire body, and penalties were imposed for disobeying such deterrent rules. They were restricted in movement and participation in governance from society as well as their own homes.

The US entered Afghanistan at the time when the Taliban refused to repatriate. Its mission stood for nation building and to improve lives of women and girls was the fundamental focus and agenda. The Constitution guaranteed the rights and also quotas to be a part of politics, and women can also join in different sectors of work areas such as army, police forces, television presenters, etc.

Even though on the path of growth, as per the polls about 90 per cent of women experience abuses in their lifetime in Afghan in terms of criminal offences. The growth is completely restricted in rural areas which were following the traditional laws of Islam. The United States' leverage to preserve at least some of their rights and privileges is limited and diminishing. But it had zero impact, hence the US must exercise whatever leverage it has remaining to preserve the rights and protect the needs of Afghan women.

It's observed that since the United States has pulled out its military presence in Afghanistan, it has given a strong reason to the Taliban to remain in power, which has given reason to negotiate war between Afghan Government and the Taliban. But with this massive takeover emerges the question of the fate of women as well as their rights.

Attack on Women in Public Life

Late 20th century, to be precise in 1964, Afghan constitution provided equal rights to both genders, therefore women could enter the house of representatives and were also given opportunity to be in position of power during the presidency of Revolutionary Council. Accordingly, the participation of women as parliamentarians and other officials were enhanced.

During 1978 Afghanistan was trapped in Cold War politics with emphasis on social reforms which included making education for girls compulsory and also application of a minimum age for girls to marry. But it did not take long before efforts to impose communist ideology provoked a widespread rebellion. Within a few months the country was flooded with more than 100,000 Soviet troops. This was the beginning of the worst period for Afghan women. And this time the populist warlords used all measures available to appeal to the majority of their soldiers, and the treatment of Afghan women was placed in the hands of poorly educated, rural traditionalists. During this phase of Afghan Civil war there was no consideration of rule of law and widows were reduced to begging, rape was commonplace, and suicide among despondent women became ever more frequent.

It was in this chaotic environment in the early 1990s that the Taliban managed to extend their authority across the country. They achieved this through a combination of bribery and force of arms. They promised an alternative that, while distasteful to many Afghans, at least appeared better and more stable than civil war. But this brought little or no reprieve for Afghan women.

Considering the notion which has arisen from *pashtunwali*, which is a traditional code in which many policies that the Taliban advanced are more restrictive and more rigid to be followed than the rigid interpretations of the *Shariah* (Islamic law) require. As the Taliban became encouraged with their military victories, the dilemmas of Afghan women grew more in the territory under their control. Before long, the Taliban had taken the most traditional elements of their society and asserted that it is based on Qur'an and institutionalised them as law.

Girls' access to education after the age of eight was outlawed; women were forbidden from working; women were forced to cover their entire bodies when in public, including their faces; they were forbidden from seeking treatment from a male doctor unless accompanied by a male family member; they were forbidden from speaking loudly in public; their voices were banned from the radio; and it was made illegal to display any images of women, either in public or in the home.

Untold numbers of educated women, who had previously worked as productive members of the society, were concealed behind burqas and removed from public life. Others were reduced to begging or prostitution in order to provide for their families. They were considered as commodities and treated with brutality such as whipping for sex outside of marriage, stoning them to death for certain offences and punishment for not wearing burqa.

Lack of Protection

In considering the moderation behaviour it is the Taliban in power which restricted the formal rights as per the rights which were enshrined to Afghan women. It has impacted the social, economic, and political conditions due to Jihadi groups, and the biased Shariah justice due to delays, paralysis and corruption after the takeover of the Taliban.

When women are threatened it's difficult to receive protection due to a weak system. In fact, women do not approach Afghan security services for help because they doubt that they would be taken seriously. In case any women raised their voices, then the authorities' response was and is usually nil, who instead of taking some action to protect them, suggested to them to not create enemies if they wanted peace and security.

Peace and order are essential parts of human dignity and need to be maintained. However, there have been numerous instances where regular threats were received with respect to killing and issues with respect to women's rights. But Afghan women are afraid to approach the police leading one to ponder a number of questions pertaining to protection and support to women and girls in Afghanistan under the Taliban. First, you need to support the corrupt government otherwise you will not be given any support. The human rights of women are violated rampantly due to failure on the part of Government. The glaring example is the case of Zakia Zaki, a journalist and feminist activist, who was assassinated in her home in the year 2007 because she didn't stop talking and raising voices on women's issues and she didn't remain silent against this oppression. This incident made all to think seriously about the profession of a journalist.

In a similar incident, a woman police officer Hassina (not her real name) received threats from the insurgent groups such as the Taliban, and she approached the higher police authorities for support and protection as it creates a challenge to live with dignity. However, she did not get the requisite support from the higher police authorities. Instead, intervention by Human Rights Commission got some relief when Dr. Soraya Sobhrang, Women's Protection and Development Commissioner of the Afghanistan Independent Human Rights Commission (AIHRC), took a call regarding the protection and safety of all women police officers.

Women's Participation in Afghanistan (Before Intrusion of Taliban)

Afghan women's struggle for their rights can be traced from 19th century, which is long before the rise of the Taliban in the early 1990s. There were substantial conflicts between ethnic groups, between urban and rural populations of Afghanistan. On the one hand, today's activists can point to a long tradition of successful Afghan reformers, including such figures as Mahmud Beg Tarzi (1865-1933), who served as Minister of Foreign Affairs and was the father-in-law to the ruler of Afghanistan, Amanullah Khan (ruled from 1919 to 1929). On the other hand, the movement has been in conflict with a proud cultural heritage that deeply values female modesty and chastity as a part of a family's honour. Like in any other part of the world, in Afghanistan too, the most important part of the identity of any individual is their family, and its honour is important and critical in defining their position in the society. Accordingly, many Afghans for these reasons, even though they oppose the Taliban vehemently, find the westernisation of Afghanistan to be extremely dangerous and more offensive shift/trend.

The movement for women's rights in Afghanistan, in many important ways, started during the rule of Amir Abdur Rahman Khan, who was a brutal military ruler and for his tyrannical rule was known as the "Iron Amir". He executed or exiled a number of the local nobles, relocated forcibly many tribes across the state and vanquished the last "Hindu" Afghans of Kafiristan and forcibly converted them to Islam.

Sexual Violence (New Shariah Law)

Women in Afghanistan have remained recipients of sexual violence even prior to intrusion of the Taliban due to the patriarchal norms adhered to by the civilisation. Pursuant to initial ruling of the Taliban after 2001, women were entitled to several benefits such as participation in socio-political spheres, standing alongside men in society, etc. The mentality of men and society did not really change, while the empowerment of women had just begun to rise the Taliban again took over the governance recently in 2021. Generations who lived through their previous rulings are well aware of the stricter interpretation of Shariah during previous ruling of the Taliban in Afghanistan. Although Shariah is based out of the Quran, Ijma, the Sunnah and Qiyas the interpretation of the Taliban has remained stricter. The differences in the interpretations of Shariah are evident from the different legal norms followed by Islamic countries. The moral and spiritual guidance proffered by Shariah is overlooked by the Taliban, as a result gross violation of women's rights is observed in Afghanistan.

Present Taliban leaders have expressed liberal views for education and mobility of women and girls in Afghanistan, however incidents of violence have been reported recently. In the past, women and girls could not really appear in courtrooms and public forums without male escorts. Incidents of sexual violence were dealt with severely during execution of matters involving adultery, moral crimes, sexual harassment, etc., wherein brutal and abusive examination of body of women remained part of legal proceedings. Although promises are being made by the Taliban and political leaders' liberal interpretation of Shariah now, the actual scenario has not been changed. The complexities of interpretations and advanced nuances of Shariah norms may prima facie look calming the concerns of women, the deterrent procedures involve sexual harassment as well as violence against women and girls in Afghanistan. As the mindset of the executing authorities are also not much developed, it is hard to expect preservation of human rights of women and girls in Afghanistan while the so-called novel Shariah is implemented.

Forced and Child Marriage

Forced and Child Marriage is rampant in Afghanistan. As per one of the surveys, approximately 57% per cent of all marriages in Afghanistan fall into the category of child marriages by UNIFEM (under the legal age of 16), and approximately 70 to 80 per cent of the marriages are forced marriages. These marriages are one of the most significant contributors of the rampant domestic violence against women in Afghanistan. Further, the early marriages often contribute to girls dropping out of school, leading to lack of education amongst the women and to early childbearing, with the correlated risks of health complications leading to a number of maternal deaths.

The attitude in rural parts of the country is that they advocate marriage of girls soon after attaining the age of puberty which gets further aggravated by the poor economic conditions thereby leading to prevalence of child marriage. Children have little choice on their partner and marriage

age with much less autonomy for girls, where much less importance is given to the continuance of their education. In case of any attempts to avoid or escape forced marriages, the response of the communities and families to that are very harsh, including honour killings.

The pending Law regarding Elimination of Violence against Women in its present form, though it addresses some of the issues, including criminalising child marriage, the people and organisations working for the rights of women believe that changes in the law may lead to only minor improvements in the conditions of women. The real change would come if the attitude of the families, communities and society at large is changed, which is of utmost importance. However, that would take a long-term commitment and serious approach from the government functionaries, community and tribal leaders and influential people, NGOs and religious leaders.

Access to Justice

The underlying problem towards the misery of women in Afghanistan is the difficulty in their access to justice. The police in the country are also ill-trained as far as skill in handling gender-based violence or women's rights are concerned, as their training has been largely focused towards security and counter-insurgency rather than crime prevention, community policing and crime solving. Further, the cultural prejudices and social stigma attached to women raising voice prevent them from accessing the police or the courts of the country.

In addition, the women face discrimination, oppression and prejudice in the police stations and the courts by the officials who are rudimentary in their approach and do not have the knowledge and will to implement the law, but instead penalise the women according to the customary law, that places great emphasis on the false notion of female honour and chastity. The majority of women in jail are charged with either extramarital sex or with "running away"—something that is not a crime in Afghan law or Shariah but often reflects a fundamental rudimentary view that considers women as property of men, that is, fathers or husbands. One widely welcomed policy response to this was the creation of female-staffed

"Family Response Units" (FRUs) in police stations. However, there are serious problems with the implementation of FRUs, including insufficient numbers of women police officers and inadequate training, mentoring, and facilities.

International Treaties and National Regime to Protect the Rights: Women's Access to Justice

Globally the rights of women and girls have been well recognised and the same is evident from international instruments enumerating principles of governance to bestow protection to women and girls. The deliberations for protection of women's rights can be found from below mentioned international as well as national instruments applicable to Afghanistan:

- **United Nations—1945**

  It is the foundation of the UN which emphasises equality between men and women as is enshrined in 1945. The charter sets the goal regarding affirming faith in Fundamental Human Rights. It emphasises to promote equality without distinction to race, sex, language or religion and provides respect for basic rights and freedoms.

- **Universal Declaration of Human Rights—1948**

  This declaration was also adopted with an objective to provide equal entitlements to women and men without any distinction of any kind. This is universally applicable and provides for the basic human dignity to all human irrespective of their sex, religion, colour and race, that is to say, it excludes all kinds of discrimination and promotes human rights and values.

- **International Covenant on Economic, Social and Cultural Rights and International Covenant on Civil and Political Rights 1966**

  After UDHR these two international covenants came into existence for attaining the objectives to provide equal opportunities and legally binding on states to meet the obligations which is laid down in the treaties. These were formulated to promote social, economic, cultural and political rights of human beings without discrimination of any kind.

- **Declaration on the Elimination of Discrimination against Women**
  It has been adopted in 1967 by UN which emphasises elimination of any kind of discrimination against women and to consider any such action to discriminate as an offence against humanity in terms of human dignity. Accordingly, such laws, customs, practices need to be curtailed which in any form lead to hindrance of the growth of women. This convention also focuses on trafficking to certain groups of women where they are restricted from enjoying their rights to the fullest.
- **Regional or National Code: Afghan Code**
  The three major legal statues enlisting legal provisions assuring legal protection to women in Afghanistan are inscribed here below:
  A. Constitution 2004—Afghan Constitution under Article 22 provides for the equality to both men and women.
  B. Afghan Civil Code 1977—It provides rights for women to inherit or own the property. It also sets the minimum age for marriage and provides women's right to choose the partner and to initiate marital separation.
  C. The Afghan Criminal Code 1979—It protects the women from any kind of domestic violence.

Violation of Human Rights of Afghan Women

There is a requirement that various leaders and authorities of Muslim Nations intervene to protect the rights of Afghan women. The Taliban in Afghanistan has deprived women of access to education, jobs, and healthcare. The Taliban has not been able to clearly define and stipulate the requirement for the women to work and choose their profession and as to what is meant by the condition that women will be allowed to work "within the framework of Islamic law". Apart from this a number of other issues have emerged which are in violation of their basic rights in which girls are affected, such as ban on secondary education and orders to female government employees to stay home. Further, the Ministry of Women's Affairs which was tasked with protecting women's political and civil rights has now been replaced by the feared "Ministry for the Propagation of Virtue and Prevention of Vice".

Women have been deprived of a number of their rights, such as they are not represented in the Taliban-led interim government and Afghan women's presence in public life is not allowed. Women rights are not protected as per Doha accord that the US signed with the Taliban in February 2020. The Taliban tried to deactivate the westernisation which was ensured through the US invasion in Afghanistan. This oppression of women in Afghanistan needs an urgent intervention by leaders and other regional powers to raise their voices for enshrining the rights of Afghan Women. Whether we call it feminist war to liberalise the rights of Afghan women as they are helpless and no nation is supporting their voices. It was observed that the a few voices were raised and supported Afghan women who tried to resolve and resilience but these voices are not sufficient to uphold the gender equality in this oppressive state.

Struggle for Justice

As per the estimate of World Health Organization, almost 90% of women in Afghanistan have experienced at least one form of domestic violence, and that approximately 17% women have experienced sexual violence. The reason for this high rate of violence is rooted in cultural values which is further reinforced by the way laws are structured and the system of delivery of Justice.

Very often the women are unable to access justice on the same terms as men, whether through formal or informal dispute resolution mechanisms. For example, if an Afghan woman chooses to approach the Court for Justice under the landmark law, Elimination of Violence Against Women, she will often face violence from a family member and community people for trying to stand up for her rights. In a large number of cases, husbands, family members, police, lawyers and judges discourage women from taking legal action. There are instances of sexual assault via abusive vaginal examinations, or "virginity tests", during court procedures. The virginity examination is a routine part of criminal proceedings when women are accused of moral crimes, including sex outside of marriage, and in a number of cases women's sexual histories have been used in court as evidence to justify long prison terms.

Though both men and women face delays and a lack of support when seeking legal recourse in Afghanistan, women find it even harder because of discriminatory cultural norms and a lack of family support. These are further aggravated by the fact that the women mostly have a lower level of literacy, they lack information about how the justice system works and have very limited access to financial resources. Dependency of women on male breadwinners is also one of the most important barriers in taking legal recourse.

In addition to the above-mentioned formal obstacles, there are strong societal pressures on women to resolve marital disputes via informal justice mechanisms such as *jirgas* (an assembly of local leaders) and *shura* (a consultation process)—in spite of the fact that these mechanisms offer them very little protection. As per their customs and traditions, in these informal community dispute resolution gatherings, it is required that the women must be represented by a male family member, which further restricts their freedom to speak for themselves. Apart from these, there are some mechanisms of dispute resolution based on restorative principles, such as the exchange of women between tribes to resolve a dispute, which are fundamentally discriminatory to women.

Girls' Secondary Education

Girls' education has become the area where most of the International Communities are trying to give their support, especially after the decimation of girls' schools in Afghanistan by the Taliban. Still, the majority of girls do not even attend Primary School, only around 11% of secondary school age girls are enrolled in classes 7 to 9 and less than 4% are enrolled in grades 10 to 12. The low enrolments of girls in school for various grades would adversely affect the future of girls in many ways and would have a wide impact on women's rights and development. Education of girls often reduces the prevalence of child marriage, early childbearing, and the risk of dying due to pregnancy-related causes. Women's literacy is also linked to increased nutrition among children. Further, on the girl's education depends the foundation of the women leaders of the next generation.

Human Rights Watch research shows that a lack of girls' schools, security, transportation alternatives, female teachers, and adequate government planning all contribute to putting education out of girls' reach. National surveys have reinforced the finding that many Afghan families wish to educate their daughters, but they must first have the means to do so practically and safely. In southern and eastern Afghanistan, general insecurity and attacks on schools, teachers, and students remain the primary barriers, with a disproportionate effect on girls.

The plight of women is directly connected to far deeper problems in the Afghan political system. This includes the growing weakness of the government, which has led to an over-reliance on fundamentalist and conservative factions to maintain political support and fight the Taliban, and a correspondingly weakening commitment to providing leadership on women's rights. Civil servants often see little to gain in pushing for women's empowerment and development, particularly if doing so risks resistance or worse from powerful factions.

However, denying Afghan women the right to education and work is an insult to their dignity which also deprives the country of the energy and talent of half of its population. As such, it is a recipe for further political instability, societal strife and economic chaos. Further, the indifference of Muslim leaders to the Taliban's rollback of women's rights is nothing but a slap in the face of millions of empowered Muslim women who are active and fully-fledged citizens of their countries. Allowing the Taliban a free pass to pursue their oppressive agenda is also an unfortunate stamp of approval for the militant group's unique mix of cruel, tribal, and restrictive interpretation of Islamic law.

Finally, leaving issues of women's rights—and generally questions of rights and freedoms—to Western countries allows the Taliban to discredit such concerns as part of a Western agenda to superimpose their Western culture. With their oppressive and retrograde outlook, giving the Taliban more time to define their views and vision for Afghanistan and the role of women is not at all an option. Muslim women across the world are speaking up. They include Nobel Laureate and Pakistani rights activist Malala Yousafzai, shot at by the Taliban in Pakistan in 2012, who has urged Pakistan to show "bold and strong commitment" to protect women's rights in Afghanistan because the Taliban ideology "can harm the whole region". Fawzia Koofi, Afghanistan's first woman deputy speaker of parliament, has asked Muslim countries to press the Taliban on girls' education, "because what is happening in Afghanistan differs from the rest of the Islamic world".

International Treaties

The Quran, the holy book of Islam, also provides that Muslims must be faithful to any treaties and contracts they enter into. Afghanistan as a sovereign nation has ratified several key international treaties relating to individual rights and liberties. These treaties include the Convention on the Political Rights of Women of 1953, which provides that women shall have all the political rights that are afforded to men, including the right to vote in all elections as well as the right to run for the elections, and to hold any public office. Afghanistan was one of the first nations to ratify this treaty. Afghanistan is also a signatory to the International Covenant on Economic, Social, and Cultural Rights and the International Covenant on Civil and Political Rights. Both of these covenants provide that the enumerated rights shall be granted equally without regard to sex, religion, or race. These two treaties provide rights in broad areas and because Afghanistan has ratified these agreements, they provide Afghan women equal legal rights as to men in those areas. Afghanistan is also a member of the International Labour Organization and ratified the Convention Concerning the Equal Remuneration for Men and Women Workers for Work of Equal Value of 1951, which provides that men and women must earn equal pay for equal work. Moreover, Afghanistan ratified the Convention Concerning Discrimination in Respect of Employment and Occupation of 1958, which provides that parties agree to undertake programmes to stem all discrimination (both race and sex-based) with respect to employment.

Flaws in the Taliban System: Return to Taliban Rule

Though the situation in Afghanistan has been difficult for women over the past two decades, there was at least a tilt in the positive direction and support for improvement in the condition and rights of the women, among many sections of the society. However, the justice system operated by the Taliban, by contrast, is likely to wilfully violate the constitutional and international protections that are in place to support women. With the international community in denial mode, there will be no one to stop the new regime from dismantling these protections. It took significant political pressure to push ahead with what reforms have taken place till now, that will now disappear altogether.

One major concern is the future of the many women's rights organisations and other civil society groups that have been operating in Afghanistan until now. International charities and foreign embassies who have supported their work on the ground but are now leaving them vulnerable.

The Afghan legal system is highly complex and biased. It is based on religious values, custom and tribal values, often resulting in discriminatory processes. For example, Women can be imprisoned for *zina* (moral crimes) that can include "running away from home" in domestic violence cases. Even when a court rules in favour of a woman, she may still face violence at the hands of her own family. Patriarchal norms and sociocultural values carry a great deal of weight and often prevent women from accessing the public sphere—such as courts and police stations—without the accompaniment of male guardians. Taking legal action against spouses is often perceived as a shameful taboo. These practices continue despite two decades of progress. Now it seems more likely that such practices will become the norm under the Taliban. Their recent statement declares: "We are going to allow women to work and study within our frameworks." The big question here is: what is the framework being offered? The women who lived under the Taliban 20 years ago remember with fear their extreme interpretation of Shariah law. These women have little faith that the new regime will be any different.

Way Forward

There has been a measurable improvement in Afghan women's rights, and their position in Afghan society in the years since the Taliban were defeated in late 2001. In urban areas, women have better access to education, they have returned to the work force, and some Afghan women have been politically outspoken and active in their nation's governance. There now exists a Ministry of Women's Affairs, women have been appointed to high government posts, they have the right to vote, and women have been elected as representatives to the Loya Jirga, Afghanistan's Grand Council.

These are only small steps in recovering from the damages of the past three decades, and efforts to move ahead are full of resistance. This resistance is partly due to the influence of the people with a traditional approach and partly due to a widespread desire to resist westernisation—even among those who consider themselves to be moderates and reformers.

But in thinking about the future of Afghan women, it is important to recognise that there is an established historical precedent for reform within Afghanistan—indeed, for most of the twentieth century the story is one of gradual progress and improvement in women's lives.

Towards this end, it is very important that members of not only the Constitutional Commission, but the Judicial Commission and Human Rights Commission address opposition to women's legal rights in the new Constitution of Afghanistan. This can be done by:

- Framing the issue of women's rights as one of human rights and the protection from unfair discrimination for all of Afghanistan's citizens;
- Utilising support in Islamic law and philosophy to show that legal protection of gender equality and equity is as per the norms of Islamic law and history and with Islamic principles of protecting human rights, promoting justice, and fairness; and
- Utilising support in Afghan law, including protection in past constitutions and international treaties to which Afghanistan is a party, to show that legal protection of gender equality and equity is not alien to the history or culture of Afghanistan.

Conclusion and Key Recommendations

It must be recalled by the Taliban and its officials and also the government of Afghanistan that Afghanistan is a party to the Convention on the Prevention of the Crime of Genocide, the International Covenant on Civil and Political Rights, the International Covenant on Economic, Social and Cultural Rights, the Convention against Torture and Other Cruel, Inhuman or Degrading Treatment or Punishment, the Convention on the Rights of the Child, and the Geneva Convention relative to the Protection of Civilian Persons in Time of War, and that it has signed the Convention on the Elimination of All Forms of Discrimination against Women. In spite of the above treaties, it's a matter of deep concern that there are deteriorating economic and social conditions of women and girls in all areas of Afghanistan, in particular in areas under the control of the Taliban movement. There are reports of grave violations of the human rights of women and girls, including all forms of discrimination against them, such as restrictions on access to health care, to many levels and types of education, to employment outside the home and, at times, to humanitarian aid, as well as restrictions on their freedom of movement.

There is a need to sincerely welcome the ongoing work of the Special Rapporteur of the Commission on Human Rights on the situation of human rights in Afghanistan, in particular his special focus on violations of the human rights of women and girls, especially in territories under the control of the Taliban faction. Also, the work of inter-agency gender mission to Afghanistan in November 1997, conducted by the Special Adviser to the Secretary-General on Gender Issues and Advancement of Women, taking into account the report of the mission and hoping that the mission will serve as a model for future efforts to address the gender dimension of crisis/conflict situations, requires to be credited.

The international community's support of and solidarity with the women and girls of Afghanistan, being supportive of the women of Afghanistan who protest against violations of their human rights, and encouraging women and men worldwide to continue efforts to draw attention to their situation and to promote the immediate restoration of their ability to enjoy their human rights requires appreciation.

The oppressive mindset of the Taliban and inaction at the level of government of Afghanistan needs to be condemned for the continuing grave violations of the human rights of women and girls, including all forms of discrimination against them, in all areas of Afghanistan, particularly in areas under the control of the Taliban. Also to be condemned are the restrictions on women's access to health care and the systematic violation of the human rights of women in Afghanistan, including the restrictions on access to education and to employment outside the home, freedom of movement, and freedom from intimidation, harassment and violence, which has a serious detrimental effect on the well-being of Afghan women and the children in their care.

It is very earnestly urged to the Taliban and other Afghan parties to recognise, protect, promote and act in accordance with all human rights and fundamental freedoms, regardless of gender, ethnicity or religion, in accordance with international human rights instruments, and to respect international humanitarian law. Further, all the Afghan parties, in particular the Taliban, are urged to bring to an end without delay all human rights violations against women and girls and to take urgent measures to ensure:

- The repeal of all legislative and other measures that discriminate against women and girls and those which impede the realisation of all their human rights;
- The effective participation of women in civil, cultural, economic, political and social life throughout the country;
- Respect for the equal right of women to work and their reintegration in employment;
- The equal right of women and girls to education without discrimination, the reopening of schools and the admission of women and girls to all levels of education;
- Respect for the right of women to security of person and that those responsible for physical attacks on women are brought to justice;
- Respect for freedom of movement for women;
- Respect for women's and girls' effective and equal access to the facilities necessary to protect their right to the highest attainable standard of physical and mental health;
- Respect for women's and girls' existence and womanhood;
- Assurance of non-violence to physical and mental wellbeing of women and girls;
- Encouragement to women empowerment and leadership within the country.

There is a need to encourage the continuing efforts of the United Nations, international and non-governmental organisations and donors to ensure that all United Nations-assisted programmes in Afghanistan are formulated and coordinated in such a way as to promote and ensure the participation of women in those programmes and that women benefit equally with men from such programmes. Further, there is an appeal to all States and to the international community to ensure that all humanitarian assistance to the people of Afghanistan, in conformity with the Strategic Framework for Afghanistan, is based on the principle of non-discrimination, integrates a gender perspective, and actively attempts to promote the participation of both women and men and to promote peace and respect for human rights and fundamental freedoms. Further, it is urged that the States must give special attention to the promotion and protection of the human rights of women in Afghanistan and to maintain a gender perspective in all aspects of their policies and actions related to Afghanistan.

In addition, there is sincere request to the Secretary-General of United Nations to ensure that all United Nations activities in Afghanistan are carried out according to the principle of non-discrimination against women and girls, and that a gender perspective and special attention to the human rights of women and girls are fully incorporated into the work of the civil affairs unit established within the United Nations Special Mission to Afghanistan, including the training and selection of staff, and that efforts be made to enhance the role of women in preventive diplomacy, peace-making and peacekeeping.

References

"Lenos leading effort to help Afghan Women", CNN-Showbuzz. March 29, 1999.

Allan Nacheman, "Afghan women tell tales of brutality, terror at hands of Taliban", AFP, May 3, 2001.

Amnesty International, "Women in Afghanistan: The violations continue", June 1, 1997. Accessed from the original on November 19, 2006.

BBC News, "Jolie urges aid for Afghan plight", BBC, May 8, 2005.

Bureau of Democracy, Human Rights, and Labor, "Afghanistan Country Report on Human Rights Practices for 1997", US Department of State, January 30, 1998.

Daniel Victor, "Explained: Shariah Law, and what it means for Afghan women", *New York Times*, August 27, 2021.

Hillary Clinton, "New Hope for Afghanistan's Women", *Time*, November 4, 2001.

Sunita Mehta (ed.), *Women for Afghan Women: Shattering Myths and Claiming the Future* (Palgrave Macmillan, 2002). ISBN: 1-4039-6017-8.

Nasrine Gross, "Afghan Women's Request for Recognition at the U.N.", 2007.

Abdullah Qazi, "The Plight of the Afghan Woman", December 9, 2010.

RAWA, "Restrictions Placed on Women by the Taliban", 2008.

Revolutionary Association of the Women of Afghanistan (RAWA), "Afghan woman stoned to death for adultery", March 30, 1997.

Sahar Maranlou, "View: Progress on women's rights has been hard fought—now everything is at risk under the Taliban", *The Economic Times*, August 23, 2021.

Rosemarie Skaine, *The Women of Afghanistan under the Taliban* (MacFarland & Company, 2002). ISBN: 0-7864-1090-6.

"The Taliban's War on Women: A Health and Human Rights Crisis in Afghanistan" (PDF), Physicians for Human Rights, 1998. ISBN: 1-879707-25-X.

The UN Refugee Agency, "Chronology of Events January 1995-February 1997".

UNFPA, "Afghan NGOs Provide Maternal Care Despite Shortage of Skilled Staff", 002.

UNICEF, "At a glance: Afghanistan", 2003.

Women of Afghanistan in the Post-Taliban Era: How Lives Have Changed and Where They Stand Today (MacFarland & Company). ISBN: 978-0-7864-3792-4.

10. The Resistance of Panjshir in the Face of the Taliban

Vibhaa Sreedhar

Introduction

A look at the history of Afghanistan would give us a better idea of how the resistance of Panjshir has evolved. Prior to 9/11, this was the scenario: The Taliban controled the majority of Afghanistan, but not all of it.[1] In contrast to the situation at present, when they appear to have expanded their grip beyond the Panjshir Valley; earlier, they only held Kandahar to Kabul in the 1990s, and even then, Herat and the North fought back hard. Herat fell ultimately, but the North, headed once again by the Panjshir Valley, Ahmad Shah Massoud, and the Northern Alliance, had their own autonomous territory that the Taliban were never able to overrun.[2] As a result, Afghanistan was divided between the Northern Alliance in the north and the Taliban in the south, with the latter establishing the Islamic Emirate.[3] Only Pakistan, Saudi Arabia, and the United Arab Emirates had accepted the Taliban as the legitimate government of Afghanistan.[4] They do, however, tumble in 2001, and do so very swiftly.[5]

The Taliban and Northern Alliance warlords were the main fighting parties in Afghanistan from 1994 until the US invasion in late 2001, and their armed forces fought each other on the frontlines.[6] Once hostile to each other, the Northern Alliances—an ethnic collation of Tajik Jamiat-e-Islami "Islamic Society" party under Burhanuddin Rabbani, the Panjshiri Shura-e-Nezar party, "supervisory council of the north" under Ahmad Shah Massoud, the Hazara Wahdat-Islami "Islamic Unity" party led by Abdul Ali Mazari and the Jumbish-e-Mili of General Dostum—was formed after the capture of Kabul by the predominantly Pashtun movement of the Taliban in September 1996.

The US had no valid reason to stay in the region when the Soviets left, therefore the destiny of key Sunni Islamic Mujahideen parties was handed over to the US's major allies, Pakistan and Saudi Arabia. Pakistan supported Gulbuddin Hekmatyar's Hezb-e-Islami (the Islamic Party), a largely Pashtun ethnic party, and gave it financial and military backing to overthrow the Rabbani-Massoud administration in Kabul. As the Hezb-e-Islami party, led by Hekmatyar, demonstrated inefficiency in attaining Pakistani aims over time, the Taliban emerged as the best alternative for Pakistan to invest in.[7]

Meanwhile, the Rabbani-Massoud regime relied heavily on military and financial help from India, Iran, and Russia. In 1994, a small group of Madrasa (religious schools) students, known as the "Taliban", mobilised by their instructors—ex-Mujahideen who had fought against the Soviets in the 1980s and had continued their education in Madrasas after the war ended—rebelled against the atrocities and "lawlessness" of local warlords in the southern Kandahar province. The Taliban were then organised to destabilise Kabul's Tajik-led administration. Although there is no question that the Pakistani military and ISI supported the Taliban from the start, it is unclear when and how this backing began, and whether the Taliban were a self-emerging entity from the start.[8]

At first, the Taliban promised to put an end to warlordism's cruelty and to bring peace and stability to Afghanistan. As a result, the new movement quickly won the hearts and minds of the Pashtun-dominated populace in southern Afghanistan, which had been subjected to years of conflict and brutality. The Taliban's first move was to renounce warlordism and disband all militia members. Those who surrendered were given their arms back to govern, and they swept up district after district and province after province until 1996, when their heavily armed men arrived on the outskirts of Kabul. It's worth emphasising that the Taliban were successful in bringing stability and putting an end to the warlords' lawless savagery throughout the region they controlled. The circumstances that they later placed on regular residents, however, were suffocating and inhumane.[9]

On September 27, 1996, they captured Kabul and swiftly moved towards the north. By the mid-1998, the Taliban controlled almost 90% of the Afghan soil, squeezing the Northern Alliance's militias to a limited territory in the north.[10] Pakistan recognised the Taliban administration as "the genuine Afghan government" in 1997, and Saudi Arabia and the United Arab Emirates followed suit soon after. The Taliban took off their hero mask after capturing Kabul, declaring Afghanistan an Islamic Emirate and enforcing their version of "Islamic Sharia law", a distinct type of violence based on an ultra-conservative and literal interpretation of the Quran. In all parts of the country, the Emirate established a Sharia police agency called "Amr-eBelmaruf wa-Nah-e-Anel-Munkar", which literally means "the order to do good and desist from doing wicked or illegal."[11]

The Islamic Emirate forbade women from participating in social activities such as going to school and working in the government or commercial sector. Long beards were mandated for men. Photography, videos, and music were strictly forbidden, and anyone who disobeyed the regulations were publicly shamed. For suspected disobedience of Sharia law, the Sharia police held self-styled street courts, in which men and women were lashed, beaten, and shot. Taliban forces faced violent resistance from the Shia minority in Hazarajat areas, particularly in Bamyan, as well as Uzbek warlords, between 1998 and 2001. They began to apply sharia law, flogging, beating, and chopping off hands and fingers as the days passed, and a new horror crept over Kabul's town and streets.[12]

According to a Human Rights Watch study, the Taliban ruthlessly massacred almost 2,000 civilians, predominantly Hazara and Uzbek ethnics, when they retook Mazar-e-Sharif for the second time in 1998. In revenge, General Dostum's militiamen smothered and shot dead roughly 3,000 Taliban detainees in shipping containers in a 2001 US-backed operation. The ethnic hatred of Pashtuns toward Tajik, Hazara, and Uzbek in the north and the rest of the country was greatly exacerbated by these atrocities and war crimes. They also aided the recruitment of Pashtun allies for the Taliban attack in the south and east, as well as in northern Afghanistan, in subsequent years. Similarly, poppy cultivation and trade grew across the country, providing not only a better life for local farmers but also a significant source of government revenue through the imposition of taxes and tolls on farmers. At the request of the international community during their last year of power, the Taliban banned the cultivation and trade of opium in the areas remaining under their control. Shortly after their fall in late 2002, the re-emerging Taliban insurgency not only allowed but supported the poppy cultivation in the areas of their control, which motivated local farmers and traders to support the re-emergence of the Taliban after US invasion.[13] During their final year in power, the Taliban banned the cultivation and trade of opium in the territories still under their control, at the request of the international community. Shortly after their fall in late 2002, the resurgent Taliban insurgency not only allowed but encouraged poppy production in regions under their control, motivating local farmers and traders to back the Taliban after the US invasion.[14]

The US military action in Afghanistan after 9/11 could be justified solely on the basis of "self-defense" and "security" concerns.[15] The Taliban Emirate's unwillingness to hand over 9/11 suspect Osama bin Laden, the leader of the Al Qaeda terrorist organisation, prompted the United States to launch a war on terror (against Al Qaeda and the Taliban for providing it with safe haven) and subsequently invade Afghanistan. Another justification for the US invasion is based on the moral logic of the cosmopolitan theory, which authorises international military involvement when a state or regime causes human suffering to its own people. That argument was made even before the 9/11 attacks, and the Taliban regime was already being scrutinised by international forces in preparation for a possible intervention due to its violent and oppressive rule and human rights violations against its own people, including a ban on women's education.[16]

Even before 9/11, Afghanistan desperately needed a state-building intervention. When the Bush administration declared war on terror (Al Qaeda) and its safe havens (the Taliban government), there was no strategy or plan for a subsequent nation-building and state-building campaign in Afghanistan. The goal of the Bonn process was to fill the power vacuum left by the Taliban's removal. It's also worth noting that, unlike Iraq, Japan, and Germany, Afghanistan did not have a functioning government before the US invasion. The state apparatus had been seriously damaged by a decade of war and violence (described in the previous section), and it was scarcely able to provide even basic services (for example, security, water, shelter, health, education, and the rule of law) to its people.[17]

One-quarter of the Afghan populace had migrated, while the rest were held captive by the Taliban Emirate's strict Sharia law or the Northern Alliance warlords' vicious violence. The Afghan informal governance mechanisms, which had previously been successful in settling community problems and had often served as a mediator between the state and society, have been disturbed since the emergence of the warlords in the 1990s. Similarly, the illicit economy—which includes poppy farming, drug trafficking, and illegal export and import of other items—largely benefited conflict parties and mafia organisations.[18]

Situation Post-9/11 and US Withdrawal

We are all well aware of the role the US played in rebuilding Afghanistan, their investments, training and various other measures taken to restore peace in the region. After this, the Trump administration contemplated the withdrawal of US forces in 2020.

The United States and the Taliban signed an agreement that specifies the criteria for the United States' withdrawal from Afghanistan by May 1, 2021, but two classified annexes that set the conditions for the withdrawal have yet to be released.[19] According to a Department of Defense Inspector General study, the US had around 13,000 troops in Afghanistan at the time of the deal. In an address to the Conservative Political Conduct Conference, Trump stated that the removal of US forces was contingent on the "Taliban's action against al-Qaeda and other terrorists who could threaten us." (US withdrawals happened despite reports from the Defense Department's Inspector General's office that the Taliban collaborated with Al Qaeda.) The accord called for the release of 5,000 Taliban members held captive by the Afghan government, which is not a signatory to the agreement.[20]

President Ashraf Ghani of Afghanistan opposed a clause in the agreement requiring his country to release 5,000 Taliban detainees. General

Mark Milley, Chairman of the Joint Chiefs of Staff, told the Senate Armed Services Committee that the Taliban pledged in the classified documents not to attack US soldiers or coalition forces, or to launch "high-profile attacks", such as in Afghanistan's 34 provincial capitals. "[T]he Taliban have agreed to a long list of criteria … all members of Congress have access to all of the documentation related to this agreement, …" Despite the deal, the Taliban launched an attack on Afghan forces in Helmand region, prompting an air strike by the US. Ghani ordered the release of 1,500 Taliban captives under US pressure, but at a rate of 100 per day.

Even though "the Taliban escalated hostilities further after signing the agreement", the DOD Inspector General's office noted in its quarterly report on Afghanistan that the US lowered force levels in Afghanistan by more than 4,000. As part of the US-Taliban agreement, Afghanistan freed the final 400 Taliban detainees, paving the stage for intra-Afghan peace talks to begin. Afghanistan government officials and Taliban representatives gathered in Qatar for peace talks after seven months of delays. The first round of peace talks between the US and the Taliban was supposed to start on March 10, according to the US-Taliban agreement. Taliban strikes against government forces have persisted. "Taliban attacks in three provinces across northern Afghanistan since Tuesday have killed at least 17 people, including six civilians, and injured scores more," according to Voice of America, "even as a Taliban political team was negotiating peace with Afghan government representatives in Doha, Qatar."[21]

Acting Secretary of Defense Christopher Miller announced that US personnel in Afghanistan will be reduced to 2,500 by January 15, 2021. On the same day, the Pentagon's Inspector General's office released a report for the quarter ending September 30, 2020, claiming that peace talks between Afghan government and Taliban representatives had stopped and violence had intensified. "At the same time, the Taliban upped its attacks on Afghan forces, resulting in 'distressingly high' levels of violence that could jeopardise the peace agreement," according to the assessment. After a series of false beginnings, Afghan and Taliban negotiators have agreed on a framework for peace talks. "At the same time, the Taliban continued its 'fight and talk' approach, increasing violence across the country to improve its leverage in negotiations with the Afghan government," according to a quarterly report from the Defense Department Inspector General's office.[22]

The Inspector General's report also stated that the Taliban appeared to be breaking the disengagement agreement. "This withdrawal is conditional on the Taliban adhering to the agreement's provisions, which include not permitting terrorists to use Afghan soil to harm the US and its allies," according to the report. "However, because al-Qaeda militants were integrated into the Taliban's leadership and command structure, it was unclear if the Taliban was abiding by the pact."[23]

Biden said on April 14 that all troops will be pulled from Afghanistan by September 11, stating that it is "time to stop the endless war". After a trip to Afghanistan in 2008, Biden became convinced that "more and indefinite American military force could neither produce or sustain a viable Afghan government," according to a speech explaining the decision. "To assure Afghanistan would not be used as a base from which to attack our nation again," the US achieved its initial and principal goal, and "our reasons for continuing in Afghanistan are becoming increasingly unclear."[24]

In response to Biden's decision to postpone the full withdrawal until September 11, the Taliban issued a statement saying that failing to complete the withdrawal by May 1 "allows [the Taliban] to take all necessary countermeasures, and thus the American side will be held responsible for all future consequences." Biden pushed the deadline for full troop departure to August 31, claiming that "speed is safety". Biden acknowledged that the action comes at a time when the Taliban is "at its most militarily powerful since 2001". Biden claims that if he reneged on Trump's deal, the Taliban "would have resumed their attacks on our forces" and that "staying would have resulted in U.S. troops suffering deaths." Biden reassured Americans that a Taliban takeover of Afghanistan is "not inevitable", and he denied that US intelligence predicted the Afghan government would fall apart. Despite the agreement it signed with the US, the Taliban gained control of its first province, the capital of Nimroz province in Afghanistan, on August 6. Taliban forces had entered Kabul,

Afghanistan's capital, by August 15, the Afghan president had departed the country, and the US embassy had been evacuated by helicopter.[25] And the rest of the world was watching.

The focus on the combat rather than the economic, political, and social flashpoints that gave rise to successive jihadist movements among both Sunni and Shiite Muslims, extending back at least four decades, has been a frequent error in US policy. Extremist versions of politicised Islam have typically evolved in countries plagued by poverty and high unemployment, authoritarian rule and political estrangement, sectarian or social marginalisation, and significant foreign influence.

Resistance of Panjshir

Panjshir, the last stronghold of armed resistance against the Taliban, has a reputation for being tough to conquer.[26] The debris of tanks destroyed during the long battle against the Soviet Union in the 1980s still litters the rough mountain valley. The fighting in Panjshir has been the most visible example of Taliban resistance. However, certain cities have seen small, scattered rallies for women's rights or in defence of the defeated Afghan republic's green, red, and black flag. Panjshir's opposition is rallying around Ahmad Massoud, the son of charismatic leader, Ahmad Shah Massoud. Massoud led the anti-Russian resistance effort, but he was slain by Al Qaeda members posing as journalists in 2001, just two days before the 9/11 attacks on the United States.[27] Though there have been conflicting reports of Panjshir falling to the Taliban, it cannot be denied that it has remained as the main resistance to the Taliban's rule.

Current Scenario

The Taliban announced the formation of a caretaker administration in Afghanistan, where they had reclaimed power after two decades. To fill important positions, the Taliban pulled from its inner circle, including a close ally of the Taliban founder as premier and a wanted man on a US terrorism list as interior minister. In the 33-member cabinet, Mullah Hassan Akhund has been named Prime Minister, while Sarajuddin Haqqani, the son of the Haqqani network's founder, has been named Interior Minister.

Due to his involvement in suicide attacks and affiliations to Al Qaeda, he is one of the FBI's most sought men.[28]

The Taliban appointed Mullah Hasan Akhund, a close ally of the movement's late founder Mullah Omar, as the head of Afghanistan's new government, with Mullah Abdul Ghani Baradar, the movement's political office, as deputy.[29] Mullah Mohammad Yaqoob, Mullah Omar's son, has been appointed defence minister. Mujahid told a news conference in Kabul that all of the positions are on an interim basis. It was unclear what role Mullah Haibatullah Akhundzada, the Taliban's highest leader, would play in the administration. Since the collapse of the Western-backed government and the Islamist militant movement's control of Kabul last month, he has not been seen or heard in public. For the past 20 years, Akhund, the current leader of government, has been close to Akhunzada.

Way Forward

Despite their recent military victory, the Taliban do not have access to billions of cash from their central bank and the International Monetary Fund, which would keep the government afloat during a chaotic period. As tight evacuations from Kabul's airport continue, those monies are mostly controlled by the US and foreign organisations, providing a possible bargaining point.[30] Currently, the Taliban government is unable to access nearly all of the $ 9 billion in reserves held by the Afghan central bank, the majority of which is kept by the New York Federal Reserve. Afghanistan was also set to receive $ 450 million from the International Monetary Fund on August 23, but the distribution was essentially halted due to a "lack of clarity" surrounding the acceptance of a new Afghan Administration. There is no particular structure that is being followed in Afghanistan, and the Taliban's rule, while seemingly better than the earlier Taliban era, is still a cause of concern for many. While the lack of international recognition is also a cause of worry, there is a also a doubt as to how things would pan out. Countries are connected to Afghanistan through so many means and how long would they withhold recognition? Even if they do not recognise, would the situation in Afghanistan change? Only time will tell.

Notes

1. https://www.vox.com/world/22634008/us-troops-afghanistan-cold-war-bush-bin-laden
2. Ibid.
3. Ibid.
4. Ibid.
5. Ibid.
6. https://www.db-thueringen.de/servlets/MCRFileNodeServlet/dbt_derivate_00046526/daudzai.pdf
7. Ibid.
8. Ibid.
9. Ibid.
10. Ibid.
11. Ibid.
12. Ibid.
13. Ibid.
14. Ibid.
15. https://www.db-thueringen.de/servlets/MCRFileNodeServlet/dbt_derivate_00046526/daudzai.pdf
16. Ibid.
17. Ibid.
18. Ibid.
19. https://www.factcheck.org/2021/08/timeline-of-u-s-withdrawal-from-afghanistan/
20. https://www.factcheck.org/2021/08/timeline-of-u-s-withdrawal-from-afghanistan/
21. Ibid.
22. Ibid.
23. Ibid.
24. Ibid.
25. Ibid.
26. https://theprint.in/opinion/afghanistans-panjshir-valley-the-last-resistance-to-taliban-rule/723857/
27. Ibid.
28. https://www.hindustantimes.com/world-news/taliban-forms-33-member-cabinet-in-afghanistan-full-list-101631066722518.html
29. https://www.cnbc.com/2021/09/07/taliban-name-new-afghan-government-amid-protests-in-kabul.html
30. https://www.firstpost.com/world/meet-ayman-al-zawahiri-the-al-qaeda-chief-who-owes-allegiance-to-taliban-supreme-leader-mullah-haibatullah-akhundzada-9891061.html

Index